Translation and Teaching in the Economic Field

LANGUAGE IN THE DIGITAL AGE

Series Editors:
José Ramón Calvo-Ferrer, Jose Belda-Medina,
Frederic Chaume & Kristi Jauregi-Ondarra

VOLUME 1

Daniel Gallego-Hernández (ed.)

Translation and Teaching in the Economic Field

Challenges in the Age of Machine Translation?

PETER LANG

Berlin - Bruxelles - Chennai - Lausanne - New York - Oxford

Library of Congress Cataloging-in-Publication Data
A CIP catalog record for this book has been
applied for at the Library of Congress.

Bibliographic information published by the Deutsche Nationalbibliothek.
The German National Library lists this publication in the
German National Bibliography; detailed bibliographic data
is available on the Internet at http://dnb.d-nb.de.

GENERALITAT
VALENCIANA
Conselleria d'Innovació,
Universitats, Ciència
i Societat Digital

ISSN 2940-9306
ISBN 978-3-631-91380-2 (Print)
E-ISBN 978-3-631-91381-9 (E-PDF)
E-ISBN 978-3-631-91382-6 (EPUB)
DOI 10.3726/b21499

Published by:
Peter Lang GmbH, Berlin, Deutschland

info@peterlang.com - www.peterlang.com

This publication has been peer reviewed.

Contents

List of Contributors

Julieta Amorebieta y Vera
Universidad Nacional de La Plata, Argentina

Daniel Gallego-Hernández
University of Alicante, Spain

François Maniez
Université Lumière Lyon 2, France

Darío Mantrana Gallego
Universidad de Alcalá, Spain

Danio Maldussi
Università degli Studi di Bergamo, Italy

Éric Poirier
Université du Québec à Trois-Rivières

Rana Roshdy
Dublin City University, Ireland

Daniel Gallego-Hernández

1 Business translation and pedagogy in the age of machine translation

Technological advances in the field of translation have led to the continuous development of machine translation and artificial intelligence. In the field of business translation (Gallego, 2022), these tools have achieved impressive levels of accuracy and speed, making them increasingly attractive not only to clients and professionals, but also to students. This can be inferred from recent studies on machine business translation, such as those by Shih (2013), Alcalde (2016), Peraldi (2016), Läubli et al. (2019), Fischer and Läubli (2020), Liu (2020), Martínez (2022), or Schumacher (2023). These studies have investigated the usefulness of machine translation in financial and business contexts. Their results show that machine translation can be cost-effective and, in some cases, produce translations of comparable or superior quality to human translations. However, the quality of machine translation depends on the system used, and it is important to raise user awareness of the limitations of this technology, emphasizing that the human translator remains crucial in the translation process.

In the case of business translation in the classroom, based on our experience and conversations with colleagues who teach the same specialized translation, it is not untrue that many students are lured by the apparent perfection of the results offered by such systems. The fluency and superficial quality of the translations produced often lead them to place excessive trust in these tools and to neglect essential aspects of technical translation. This lack of attention to detail can result in translations that are grammatically correct but lack conceptual accuracy. This is one of the reasons why it seems necessary to provide machine translation literacy workshops for business translation students (Bowker, 2020).

In our view, this reality poses a series of pedagogical and cognitive challenges in the training of business translators, which few studies on machine business translation, given their current focus, mention but do not elaborate on. Consequently, it is up to the reader, especially those interested in teaching, to find ways to integrate the results of such studies into the teaching of business translation in order to develop effective and productive professional skills, and to emphasize the importance of making students aware of the limitations of this technology and the centrality of the human translator in the translation process.

One of the aspects that seems to be often overlooked in the didactics of business translation is the deep understanding of business issues and the analysis of terminology and its conceptual relationships within and beyond the field. We believe this can help detect semantic- conceptual errors resulting from machine translations. If economic, business, or financial knowledge is neglected in the classroom, students may not be prepared to identify meaning problems or conceptual nuances. Lack of knowledge, combined with excessive confidence in technology, can hinder students from questioning generated translations and deepening their understanding of underlying concepts.

Given this scenario, it seems crucial to reinforce thematic knowledge in business translation classes. Indeed, students should be reminded that translation is not just a mechanical process, but an act that requires a deep understanding of the subject matter. This implies mastering specific terminology and understanding its links with other terms and basic concepts in the economic field.

Currently, there are very few studies on the didactics of business translation that include proposals that focus on subject matter expertise. It is true that BITRA (Franco, 2001–2023) lists more than 250 works on business translation and didactics, many of which emphasize the need for specialized translators to master both the terminology and the conceptual context of their field. However, it seems that thematic competence is often underestimated, with the assumption that translators acquire it on their own or through professional practice (Gallego, 2023). Gelpí (2015) is one of the very few authors who have explored methodological possibilities for the development of this competence in students. She proposes strategies to improve the thematic competence of non-specialist translators in economics. Her approach seeks to integrate thematic competence into translation, recognizing that it is different from that of an expert. Aware that proper delimitation of the subject matter of the economic text is essential, the author proposes translation-oriented thematic units to identify and understand key concepts and avoid confusion. The "Q-explanation" technique, which involves formulating questions about who, what, how, when, where, and why, is presented as an effective strategy for acquiring thematic knowledge.

Klabal and Kubánek (2019) investigate the challenges of training ecoe nomic and banking translators, and the role of thematic competence in translation skills. They examine whether exposure of translation students to professional economic discourse improves their thematic competence and translation proficiency. The study involved three groups of students: no exposure, exposure to television interviews with economists, and exposure to newspaper articles written by economists. The results show that exposure to professional discourse significantly improved translation quality, especially in developing thematic competence. Exposure to written discourse enriched terminology, while exposure to oral discourse improved overall translation acceptability. This highlights the importance of thematic competence in translator training, especially in specialized fields such as business. The authors recommend integrating professional discourse exercises into translation classes, including reading support texts, participating in debates, and completing questionnaires. They also find value in short student presentations followed by interpretation. This approach not only improves translation skills, but also keeps students abreast of current events, in keeping with the educational role of universities.

More recently, Maldussi (2023), considering that the economic-financial domain, like any other domain, has its own categories of thought, believes that the teaching challenge is to identify the notions which represent privileged access to its conceptual frameworks, as well as the peculiarities that shape its cognitive framework in relation to other specialized domains. Based on this premise, he formulates a training proposal, from an interlinguistic perspective, that helps the translator-in-training to develop an attitude that allows access to false intuitive specialized knowledge through mental exercises. The didactic goal is to make students aware of their cognitive gaps in relation to their own worldview through knowledge co-construction.

In this context, this volume brings together a selection of specific studies carried out by researchers from different parts of the world, all of whom share a common focus on business translation in relation to didactics or machine translation. These studies are from researchers who participated in the *V International Conference on Economic, Commercial, Financial and Institutional Translation,* held at the University of Alicante in June 2023. We believe that these studies offer valuable insights into the challenges of teaching business translation in the era of machine translation technology and artificial intelligence.

Rana Roshdy's chapter, "Talking business and translation: Exploring language variation in the Boston Consulting Group (BCG) matrix," examines the impact of translation on business communication and its relationship to translation approaches such as formal equivalence and dynamic equivalence as proposed by Nida (1964). It emphasizes that translation can either perpetuate or resist power imbalances between cultures, especially in contexts where the West holds a dominant position. While formal equivalence reinforces the cultural superiority of the source, dynamic equivalence promotes a multicultural approach to knowledge transfer.

In addition to emphasizing that translation is a key tool in the negotiation of cultural and linguistic transactions between dominant and less dominant cultures and can serve as a form of resistance to cultural hegemony, it prompts us to consider, in the context of the didactics of business translation in the era of machine translation and artificial intelligence, how to develop tasks or activities in the classroom that promote students' mental agility. Taking advantage of the dichotomy between formal and dynamic equivalence, several proposals come to mind.

Consider the translation of financial reports, which are typically technical and repetitive documents. Students may see them as suitable candidates for machine translation because of the generally favorable results. In this context, classroom activities could be introduced that involve "forced" or "guided translation", where students are encouraged to translate in a specific way defined by the teacher, rather than relying on their own instincts or machine-generated results. In these exercises, students would be prohibited from using literal or formal translations for certain terms, thus requiring an "awareness" of the conceptual relationships inherent in these terms. While terms such as "balance sheet," "cash flow," "income statement," "equity," "dividend," "depreciation," and various others could indeed be translated literally into other languages without disrupting the overall translation flow, the activities could also encourage alternative, non-literal, and dynamic translations that better reflect the financial context associated with each term. This, to some extent, promotes students to go beyond word-for-word translation and represent the meaning of the terminology within the translated text.

The translation of financial reports is not the only context in which this type of "forced translation" could be applied. Marketing translation provides numerous examples where student translators need to propose translations beyond literal interpretations without being forced to do so by trainers. When promoting a product in different markets and cultures, it is essential that the message be effectively adapted to reach local consumers without losing the original meaning and intent. French slogans such as "légèreté estivale" in the fashion and clothing sector, "vivre vert" in the food sector, or common recurring phrases such as "le choix numéro un" indicate that translation without prior reflection is insufficient. Even the assessment of such activities can be carried out by the students themselves, who may be enticed by the more "appealing" translation.

Dynamic equivalence need not be limited to the microtext level and can extend to the macrotext. Consider, for example, the translation of a business plan into any language pair. Recognizing the importance of taking cultural and market differences into account, the dynamic equivalence approach might involve adjusting the business strategy, product presentation, or market objectives to better match the expectations and conditions in the target market for the translation. This would undoubtedly require not only cognitive effort, but also thorough documentation, possibly leading to a collaborative project with other business students.

The second study, authored by Julieta Amorebieta and Vera from the National University of La Plata, Argentina, entitled "Problemas de equivalencia e implicancias pedagógicas de la traducción de sociedades comerciales," straddles the fields of legal and business translation. It focuses on the intricacies of translating corporate law and the resulting lack of equivalence, especially at the conceptual level. These are aspects that machine translation and artificial intelligence may fail to adequately address due to the legal and economic nuances of the countries involved. The author examines an aspect that has already been studied by other authors in different languages and countries (Orts, 2006; Gil, 2012; Monteagudo, 2021; Garrido, 2023, among others). However, her focus goes beyond the relatively understudied legal regimes of Argentina. In the context of this volume and the approach to teaching business translation in the current technological landscape, she is aware that specialized translators in business and law must have a deep understanding of the textual genres and conceptual frameworks used in the texts. Accordingly, she proposes an analytical methodology that forces translation students to outline the various characteristics and aspects of the concepts they are studying. In the present case, it refers to specific translation problems related to legal terminology and the names of legal entities in Argentina and England.

Although this methodology may be considered classical, its relevance in the current context remains crucial and its importance should be emphasized. Its implementation in the classroom can go beyond the traditional lecture, where the teacher does the analysis. Instead, it can encourage students to engage with technologies to produce a first draft (cf. Figure 1), allowing them to delve deeper into the characteristics of different business entities in different countries.

The third chapter corresponds to the study of François Maniez, entitled "Traduction automatique des trigrammes nominaux (anglais/français/anglais) dans la langue spécialisée de l'économie". The author focuses on the analysis of the translation of nominal trigrams from English to French in the field of economics. These trigrams often contain complex structures and premodifiers, making them difficult to translate automatically. The study argues that while lexicalized and high-frequency trigrams tend to be consistently translated, there is greater variability in the translation of non-lexicalized and low-frequency trigrams. This highlights the complexity of translating unusual technical terms. The study also points out that the length and structure of the noun phrase can influence the machine translation process. For example, very often if not systematically,

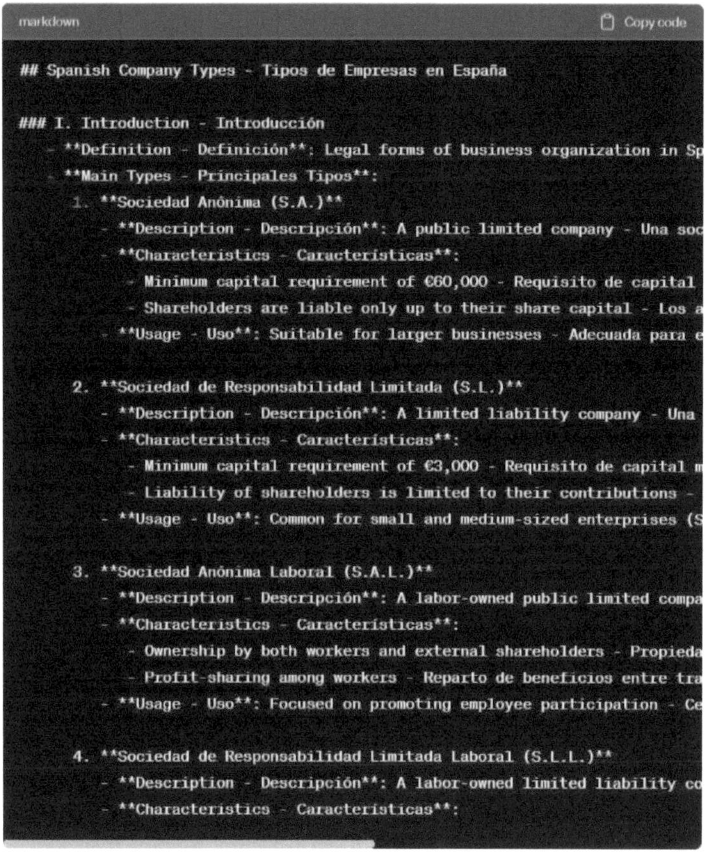

```
markdown                                                    Copy code

## Spanish Company Types - Tipos de Empresas en España

### I. Introduction - Introducción
  - **Definition - Definición**: Legal forms of business organization in Sp
  - **Main Types - Principales Tipos**:
    1. **Sociedad Anónima (S.A.)**
      - **Description - Descripción**: A public limited company - Una soc
      - **Characteristics - Características**:
        - Minimum capital requirement of €60,000 - Requisito de capital
        - Shareholders are liable only up to their share capital - Los a
      - **Usage - Uso**: Suitable for larger businesses - Adecuada para e

    2. **Sociedad de Responsabilidad Limitada (S.L.)**
      - **Description - Descripción**: A limited liability company - Una
      - **Characteristics - Características**:
        - Minimum capital requirement of €3,000 - Requisito de capital m
        - Liability of shareholders is limited to their contributions -
      - **Usage - Uso**: Common for small and medium-sized enterprises (S

    3. **Sociedad Anónima Laboral (S.A.L.)**
      - **Description - Descripción**: A labor-owned public limited compa
      - **Characteristics - Características**:
        - Ownership by both workers and external shareholders - Propieda
        - Profit-sharing among workers - Reparto de beneficios entre tra
      - **Usage - Uso**: Focused on promoting employee participation - Ce

    4. **Sociedad de Responsabilidad Limitada Laboral (S.L.L.)**
      - **Description - Descripción**: A labor-owned limited liability co
      - **Characteristics - Características**:
```

Figure 1. Output about Spanish business entities by ChatGPT

back-translation of French prepositional constructions by machine translation systems tend to be formal equivalence (construction calque with preposition) and not the more idiomatic English construction which was used in the source compound term and for which there is no similar construction in French. This suggests that machine translation may face additional difficulties when translating long and complex noun phrases in technical contexts. The study concludes that DeepL has a slight advantage over Google Translate in preserving nominal premodification in back-translation tests from French to English.

Meanwhile, the next chapter of Darío Mantrana Gallego's study, entitled "Evaluation of economic-financial DE-ES translations: A comparative study between DeepL and Google Translate," also evaluates the translation engines of DeepL and Google Translate, but this time in the language pair German-Spanish. Using a corpus of 100 economic-financial segments and their respective translations with both engines, the author applies two quality evaluation methods (manual and automatic) and three categories: accuracy, fluency and terminology. The results show that in some cases the translations are quite good (neither excellent nor disastrous), but in other cases they are not sufficient for this type of text and require pre- or post-editing because they contain significant or serious errors. The study also highlights the limitations of automatic metrics, as they do not take into account the meaning and intent of the source text, but rely on comparing matching characters, words and phrases with the reference translation.

These two studies contribute not only to the existing research on machine business translation, but also to the numerous studies on translation in general, many of which essentially evaluate machine translation systems (in this case, Google Translate and DeepL). However, for teachers interested in translation pedagogy in the current technological context, reading these studies can provide some ideas for their teaching practice, as they did for us.

Certainly, it is possible to prepare activities that compare machine translation engines, evaluate translation quality, or develop post-editing skills to critically evaluate machine translation tools and recognize when manual intervention is necessary. However, the main challenge for teachers in designing such activities is the selection of texts. According to several studies on the quality of machine translation, technical texts that are repetitive and widely available on the Internet tend to yield better results. On the other hand, more complex texts with fewer repetitions or contexts, including marketing texts, are more likely to contain errors. In this context, we consider a type of text that we have been working on for several years in the classroom and for which machine translation still does not provide adequate translations, at least in the eyes of professional translators. Table 1 contains segments of the text in question (an outdated advertisement from a defunct banking institution promoting a particular credit card). The first column includes the text segments, the second and third columns contain the machine translations by Google and DeepL, respectively, and the fourth column presents our translation. The table also includes comments from a professional business translation reviewer who reviewed all three versions. Segments of text that the reviewer found to be correct, and which he admitted he would not have thought of otherwise, are italicized. Different types of errors identified by the reviewer are underlined.

Table 1. Comparison of TM and HT

Source Text	Google MT	Deepl MT	Our Translation
Un privilegio para ti y los tuyos	Un privilège pour vous et les vôtres	Un privilège pour vous et les vôtres	Un privilège pour vous et *vos proches*
Máxima aceptación, universalidad y comodidad: la tarjeta CAM Platinum cuenta con paquetes de seguros únicos y servicios exclusivos para ti y los tuyos.	Acceptation maximale, universalité et confort : la carte CAM Platinum *propose* des forfaits d'assurance uniques et des services exclusifs pour vous et *vos proches*.	Acceptation maximale, universalité et commodité : la carte CAM Platinum *propose* des formulesd'assurance uniques et des services exclusifs pour vous et les vôtres.	Acceptée chez tous les commerçants, en Espagne et à l'étranger, 100 % confort: avec la carte CAM Platinum bénéficiez d'une gamme d'assurances unique et de services exclusifs pour vous et vos proches.
Recompensamos tus Compras con Regalos:	Nous récompensons vos Achats avec des Cadeaux:	Nous récompensons vos achats par des cadeaux:	Vos achats récompensés par des cadeaux:
Programa de Puntos. Con tus compras obtendrás un 20 % más de Puntos.	Programme de points. Avec vos achats, vous obtiendrez 20 % de Points en plus.	Programme de points. Avec vos achats, vous obtiendrez 20 % de points supplémentaires.	Programme *de fidélité. À chaque achat*, gagnez 20 % de points en plus.
Dispositivo de Telepeaje CAM VIA-T gratuito.	Dispositif de télépéage gratuit CAM VIA-T.	Dispositif de télépéage CAM VIA-T gratuit.	*Abonnez-vous gratuitement* au télépéage.

(*continued on next page*)

Table 1. Continued

Source Text	**Google MT**	**Deepl MT**	**Our Translation**
Tus viajes sin preocupaciones	Vos déplacements sans soucis	Voyage sans souci	*Voyagez l'esprit tranquille*
Tus Compras: Totalmente Protegidas	Vos achats: Entièrement protégés traduction littérale	Vos achats: entièrement protégés traduction littérale	*Achetez en toute sécurité*

Beyond the accuracy of the review, we believe that the results of such translations open up a world of possibilities for the study of this type of text in the field of business translation pedagogy in relation to machine translation.

The following study in this volume, entitled "Essential resources of Canadian origin in economic and financial translation for practicing, teaching, learning, and research purposes," was written by Éric Poirier, a financial translator with over 18 years of experience and a professor of business translation. In this study, he shares the types of resources he uses to research and prepare materials for economic and financial translation courses. On the one hand, he presents key resources from Canadian authors and organizations that have influenced the teaching and practice of economic and financial translation, with a focus on Quebec and translation from English to French. Specifically, it focuses on primary resources (monolingual and bilingual dictionaries, glossaries, and vocabularies as well as terminology databases entries), secondary resources (newsletters, analyses and comparisons of translation solutions, and encyclopedic information), and Canadian tertiary resources for economic and financial translation (comprehensive compilations that combine primary and secondary resources). On the other hand, he emphasizes terminology data sets such as TERMIUM Plus, SEDAR, thesauri of government activities, and government budgets, which provide aligned data for research and translation. He concludes his paper by referring to corpus studies, which he believes have a crucial role to play in improving the teaching of financial translation, and emphasizes the importance of combining technology with theoretical knowledge and practical skills in an increasingly globalized and technology-oriented world.

Indeed, this work can be understood as a list of Canadian resources useful for the practice, research or teaching of translation, similar to what other authors have proposed in the past (Bovy, 1964; Bergeron, 1999; Orts, 2019, among others). However, it is also true that researchers and teachers in the field of business translation, who are concerned with updating their teaching methods, can derive ideas or projects to implement in the classroom with the aim of promoting mental effort among their students. For example, Poirier mentions Dancette and Réthoré's *Analytical Dictionary of Retailing,* which he describes as "a little gem in the sub-field of marketing and commercial translation". Why not use this, or even the online *Analytical Dictionary of Globalization and Labour,* which is also an encyclopedic dictionary created by translators for translators, and develop specific activities aimed at facilitating the cultivation of cognitive abilities among aspiring translators? We believe that the author's extensive work on semantic relations (see Figure 2) can undoubtedly be used in the classroom, again with the aim of achieving a certain level of maturity in the development of thematic competence.

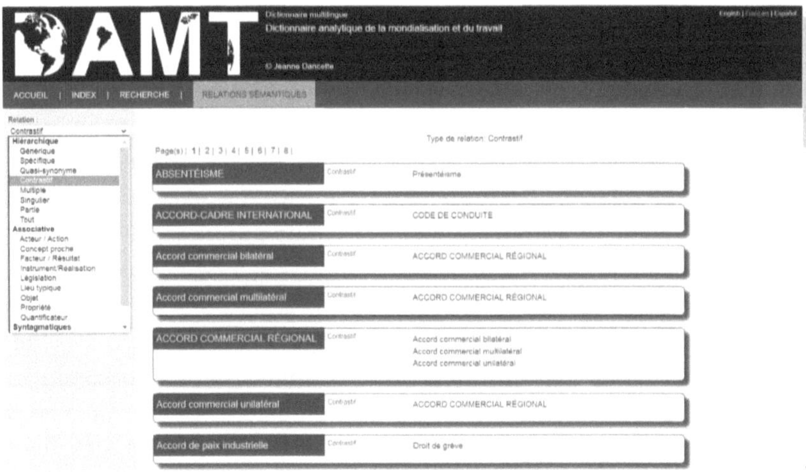

Figure 2. Semantic relationships in the *Analytical Dictionary of Globalization and Labour*

Poirier also asserts that "corpus studies will inevitably play a crucial role in enhancing the teaching and learning of financial translation, offering empirical insights and improving translation practices". The use of "will" is not accidental, in our view. Since we ourselves published a specific study on parallel texts, corpora, and economic translation (Gallego, 2012), similar works have been published that continue to advocate the use of corpora in the teaching of economic translation, but there is still a lack of empirical evidence that such resources, which seem to be not widely used in the professional field (Gallego, 2015), are actually beneficial for translation students. Why shouldn't researchers, with an interest in corpus linguistics applied to business translation, develop effective and empirically tested corpus-based methodologies that can be compared to machine translation or artificial intelligence? This step can be instrumental for both translation practice and translation education, potentially addressing the perceived stagnation in current research within this field. Undoubtedly, this presents another avenue of action that can be inferred from Poirier's statement.

The last paper in this book is by Danio Maldussi (University of Bergamo, Italy), entitled "The Lady is not tapering ou l'euphémisme en tant que figure de la médiation, entre euphémismes métonymiques et tabous". It is a study that reminds us of research by other authors who, through the conceptual analysis of certain terms (Boulanger, 2016; Boulanger & Lemieux, 2021; Stender, 2022; Galanes, 2022; among others), have essentially shown how the financial press and political discourse manipulate certain concepts according to their needs. For translation purposes, this requires a deep thematic understanding in order to effectively grasp certain moments in current political-economic events.

Specifically, Maldussi dissects the entire conceptual framework behind the neologism "tapering" in the context of European macroeconomics. This term is used to soften the reality of economic actions or policies in order to avoid negative reactions or suspicions. While Maldussi's work does not have an explicit didactic focus, it accurately describes the complexity of subject matter knowledge in economics and finance. It also illustrates how a small corpus can be used to study terminological variation in economic neology. Furthermore, it can provide insights for the creation of didactic materials that emphasize the development of this competence and highlight certain limitations or areas related to the handling of euphemistic or specialized terminology where machine translation may not perform optimally.

After reading Maldussi's work, we turned to chatGPT and requested a trilingual list of taboo economic policy terms along with their respective non-taboo forms (see Table 2). Beyond the terminological accuracy of this artificial intelligence, this small list can serve as a good starting point for working on euphemistic terminology in the classroom, in terms of who uses one version or the other. Methods can be varied, and you can even ask chatGPT for ideas. But that is a separate topic.

Table 2. Taboo terms and their non-taboo alternatives in monetary policy translation by chatGPT

Taboo Term (Spanish)	**Non-Taboo Term (Spanish)**	**Term in English**	**Term in French**
Austeridad	Disciplina fiscal	Austerity	Austérité
Rescate	Apoyo financiero	Bailout	Sauvetage
Inflación descontrolada	Incremento de precios	Uncontrolled inflation	Inflation incontrôlée
Deuda pública insostenible	Niveles elevados de deuda	Unsustainable public debt	Dette publique insoutenable
Desempleo masivo	Altas tasas de desempleo	Massive unemployment	Chômage de masse
Recorte de tipos de interés	Ajuste de tasas de interés	Interest rate cut	Réduction des taux d'intérêt
Dinero fácil	Política monetaria expansiva	Easy money	Argent facile
Intervencionismo gubernamental	Rol activo del gobierno en la economía	Government intervention	Intervention gouvernementale
Burbuja financiera	Excesiva especulación de activos	Financial bubble	Bulle financière
Estímulo fiscal	Medidas de estímulo económico	Fiscal stimulus	Stimulus fiscal

(*continued on next page*)

Table 2. Continued

Taboo Term (Spanish)	Non-Taboo Term (Spanish)	Term in English	Term in French
Bancarrota	Incapacidad de pago	Bankruptcy	Faillite
Derrumbe del mercado	Caída en los precios de los activos	Market collapse	Effondrement du marché
Evasión fiscal	Optimización fiscal	Tax evasion	Évasion fiscale
Desigualdad de ingresos	Variación en los ingresos	Income inequality	Inégalité des revenus
Crisis financiera global	Situación económica mundial	Global financial crisis	Crise financière mondiale
Manipulación de divisas	Intervención en el mercado de divisas	Currency manipulation	Manipulation des devises
Devaluación de la moneda	Disminución del valor de la moneda	Currency devaluation	Dévaluation de la monnaie
Política de ajuste estructural	Reformas económicas	Structural adjustment policy	Politique d'ajustement structurel
Quiebra bancaria	Problemas financieros bancarios	Bankruptcy of banks	Faillite bancaire
Crisis de la deuda soberana	Problemas de endeudamiento del gobierno	Sovereign debt crisis	Crise de la dette souveraine

We hope that this selection of papers proves to be of interest and offers a broader perspective on approaching the didactics of economic translation in relation to machine translation. It is evident that, in an increasingly globalized world, business translation plays a fundamental role in international communication and business decision-making. Translators must be capable of comprehending and conveying specialized concepts precisely and coherently, and this is where technologies can be a valuable tool but also an enemy.

With this book, we invite readers interested in this aspect to explore new methodologies and pedagogical approaches that emphasize the importance of developing thematic competence in business translation. The training of specialized translators in economics and commerce should address both linguistic skills and a deep understanding of economic concepts and terminology, as well as the effective integration of machine translation into the educational process.

In this chapter, we have shared some of the ideas that came to mind as we read each of the papers. Of course, readers can delve deeper into the research presented, each of which focuses on specific and valuable aspects to gain a better understanding of the business translation landscape. Ultimately, we hope that these papers will inspire new research and pedagogical approaches that will further enrich this ever-evolving field.

References

Alcalde, E. (2016). La traducción automática y el lenguaje controlado en el ámbito de la traducción financiera. In Martínez, E. et al. (Eds.), *Investigación, desarrollo e innovación universitarios* (pp. 1–9). Madrid. Ediciones Universitarias McGraw-Hill.

Bergeron, M. (1999). Ressources financières sur Internet. *Circuit, 65*: 16–17.

Boulanger, P. (2016). Quand les médias traduisent la crise. Les métaphores utilisées par la presse généraliste pendant la crise des subprimes. *Meta,* 61(Special issue): 144–162.

Boulanger, P. & Lemieux, R. (2021). Qui est 'victim*' dans les pages économiques et financières des journaux canadiens en période de crise? *Meta,* 66(3): 601–619.

Bovy, F. (1964). Le traducteur technico-commercial devant ses difficultés à la recherche de sa documentation. *Lebende Sprachen,* 9(1): 20–22.

Bower, L. (2020). Machine translation literacy instruction for international business students and business English instructors. *Journal of Business & Finance Librarianship,* 25(1–2): 25–43.

Fernández, A. (2015). La competencia documental en el aprendizaje de la traducción económica francés-español-francés. *inTRAlinea Special Issue: New Insights into Specialised Translation.*

Fischer, L. & Läubli, S. (2020). What's the difference between professional human and machine translation? A blind multi-language study on domain-specific mt. In A. Martins, et al. (Eds.), *Proceedings of the 22nd Annual Conference of the European Association for Machine*

Translation (pp. 215–224). Lisbon. European Association for Machine Translation.

Franco Aixelá, J. (2001–2023). BITRA (Bibliografía de Interpretación y Traducción). Base de datos en acceso abierto.

Galanes, I. (2022). Variación conceptual y paratraducción en la neología terminológica: eufemismo y disfemismo. In J. Yuste, & X. Garrido (Eds.), *Traducción & Paratraducción I. Líneas de investigación* (pp. 213–228). Bern: Peter Lang.

Gallego-Hernández, D. (2012). *Traducción económica y corpus: Del concepto a la concordancia. Aplicación al francés y al español.* Alicante: Universidad de Alicante.

Gallego- Hernández, D. (2015). The use of corpora as translation resources: A study based on a survey of Spanish professional translators. *Perspectives Studies in Translatology,* 23(3): 1–17.

Gallego-Hernández, D. (2020): *Traducción económica e investigación en España. Estudio bibliométrico*. Málaga. Comares.

Gallego-Hernández, D. (2022). Business translation. *ENTI (Encyclopedia of translation & interpreting)*. AIETI.

Gallego-Hernández, D. (2023). La traducción económico-financiera vista por los profesionales: Cartografía bibliográfica, *Babel,* 69(2): 159–187.

Garrido Rodríguez, I. & Piñero González, A. (2023). ¿Por qué limited liability company no (siempre) se traduce por «sociedad de responsabilidad limitada»? *Puntoycoma,* 178: 4–7.

Gelpí, C. (2015). ¿Cuánta economía debe saber el traductor? La adquisición de conocimiento temático para la traducción. *inTRAlinea Special Issue. New Insights into Specialised Translation.*

Gil, I. (2012). *La traducción en el derecho de sociedades español e inglés: estudio descriptivo, comparado y terminológico, análisis de escrituras de constitución, estatutos sociales y documentos de transferencia internacional de sede social.* Tesis doctoral. Universidad de Granada.

Klabal, O. & Kubánek, M. (2019). Enhancing thematic competence by exposure to professional discourse in economic translation. *Onomázein*, Special Issue V – Current trends in business translation: 78–93.

Läubli, S., Amrhein, C., Düggelin, P., Gonzalez, B., Zwahlen, A. & Volk, M. (2019). Post- editing productivity with neural machine translation: An empirical assessment of speed and quality in the banking and finance domain. In Forcada, M. et al. (Eds.), *Proceedings of machine translation summit XVII. Volume 1: Research track* (pp. 267–272). Dublin. European Association for Machine Translation.

Le Poder, M. (2018). Uso de corpus monolingües comparables para la traducción al francés de unidades de núcleo verbal procedentes de la sección económico-financiera del diario El País. *Babel,* 64(2): 294–325.

Liu, L. (2020). 论英汉机器翻译的改进之道— —基于《金融时报》人机翻译的比较研究 [On the improvement of the English-Chinese machine translation: Human vs. machine translation of "Financial Times" reports]. 宜春学院学报 = *Journal of Yibin University,* 1: 74–78.

López, R. (2017). Textos paralelos para la traducción económica (esp>ingl): estudio de un caso práctico extraído del aula. *Polissema – Revista de Letras do ISCAP,* 17: 163–178.

Maldussi, D. (2023). La didactique de la traduction économique et financière à l'épreuve de la sous-compétence thématique: à la recherche d'un deuxième souffle, *Meta* 68(3).

Martínez, I. (2022). La evaluación y posedición de textos económicos y financieros pertenecientes al ámbito de los organismos económicos internacionales con fines formativos. In A. Gómez, & R. Martínez (Eds.), *Translation and interpreting in institutional settings. Training and practising the profession from social and innovative perspectives* (pp. 267–286). Bern. Peter Lang.

Monteagudo, M. (2021). Análisis contrastivo de la variación denominativa dialectal y conceptual en las escrituras de constitución de las Stock corporations y las Limited liability companies estadounidenses y de las sociedades anónimas y sociedades de responsabilidad limitada peruanas. In Barceló, T. et al. (Eds.), *Tendencias actuales en traducción especializada, traducción audiovisual y accesibilidad* (pp. 177–200). Valencia: Tirant lo Blanch.

Nida, E. (1964). *Toward a science of translating.* Leiden: E.J. Brill.

Orts Llopis, M. (2006). The hidden dimension of the language of corporations in America and Spain: Perspectives for inter-legal communication. *Revista alicantina de estudios ingleses,* 19: 285–298.

Orts Llopis, M. (2019). Las obras y fuentes de referencia en la traducción especializada inglés- español, español- inglés: algunos ejemplos de soporte documental para la traducción jurídica y económica. *Hermes,* 59: 189–206.

Patin, S. (2022). A favor del uso de los corpus electrónicos en la enseñanza de la traducción. *Nueva ReCIT,* 5.

Peraldi, S. (2016). De la traduction automatique brute à la post-édition professionnelle évoluée: le cas de la traduction financière. *Revue française de linguistique appliquée,* 21(1): 67–90.

Schumacher, P. (2023). Traduction humaine et post-édition: contrôle qualité en contexte académique. *Meta,* 68(3).

Shih, C. (2013). 電腦輔助商務翻譯教學—MT及TM之案例研究 [Computer-aided business translation teaching: The use of MT and TM as aids to translation]. *Compilation and Translation Review,* 6(1): 113–146.

Stender, A. (2022). Los eufemismos de la crisis económica en la prensa especializada alemana y española. In B. Fuente, & I. Holl (Eds.), *La traducción y sus meandros: diversas aproximaciones en el par de lenguas alemán- español* (pp. 215–229). Ediciones Universidad de Salamanca.

Rana Roshdy

2 Talking business and translation: Exploring language variation in the Boston Consulting Group (BCG) matrix

Talking business requires using innovative means of linguistic expression to generate an emotional reaction. Marketing models represent a genre of business communication that caters to linguistic creativity by introducing neologisms based on giving new meanings to existing words. Not only are such neologisms intended to appeal to the reader but also to pay tribute to the firm/entity that developed the model as they are subsequently considered the owners of such signature lexis. The role of translation is problematic in this regard, particularly when the transfer occurs from a major language (an exporter of knowledge) to a minor language (an importer of knowledge). Thus, this article sets out to investigate the role of translation in business communication, questioning the extent to which translation can support or defy cultural hegemony. The article analyses two self-translated English-Arabic versions of the BCG matrix, a popular marketing model developed by an American global firm, Boston Consulting Group. The translations differ in their orientation to the source text, implementing Nida's (1964) formal and dynamic equivalence, respectively. The principal theoretical implication suggests the complex mechanisms of translating across power differentials and hegemonic positions and the need for a flipped, deep, experiential learning model for building translation competency.

Introduction

As a form of linguistic and cultural meditation among the world's countries, translation assumes an activist role in power struggle and cultural hierarchy. In contexts marked by unequal power relations, translation can grant and deprive cultures of hegemony by its conscious selection of translational approach. In the framework of communicating advances in various disciplines of human knowledge, translation can be an active participant in attributing all credit to the dominant cultures (i.e., Anglo-American cultures) through adopting source-oriented methods. Yet, it can twist the elements of the original text in a target-oriented approach to spread the word about recent developments in a way that promotes shared knowledge among all nations, cushioning the target culture against a sort of cultural colonization described as "acculturation". Here, acculturation signifies a process of interaction among cultures in the context of power relations, whereby the powerful party (the center of knowledge production) tends to forcibly impose its norms and patterns on the less powerful or the periphery. In other words, the sending culture replaces the receiving culture (Merriam-Webster, 2018). In the former scenario, the translation is in passive submission to the source culture, whereas the latter scenario spurs translation to break away from the dominance of the source lexis and syntax to defy the superiority of one culture over another. In this respect, this article discusses how in the context of translating models of knowledge dominated by English theoretical patterns into Arabic, Nida's (1964) formal equivalence aggrandizes the source culture, while dynamic equivalence empowers the target culture to strive against Western or Anglo-American hegemony. Nida's (1964) formal approach that focuses on reproducing the source content and linguistic structures in the target text emulates absolute faithfulness to the elements of the source language. Dynamic equivalence, on the other hand, permits the use of various dynamics or shifts, which are essential for adapting the foreign patterns of theorization to the target environment as well as for efficiently engaging target groups with the advancements of the other.

To reflect on the contribution of translation practice to power struggle, the article provides two different approaches to the translation of the BCG Matrix: formal and dynamic, each fulfills a respective function in the question of power. The BCG matrix represents a culture-specific marketing model whereupon its translation can either attest to the dominance of the source culture or provide a multicultural model of knowledge. While the given translations adopt either Nida's (1964) formal or dynamic equivalence per se as a method of approaching the BCG text as a whole, translation procedures developed by Vinay and Darbelnet (1958/1995) are employed to deal with minor segments or units of the text. Such distinction is attributed to Newmark (1988: 98), who posits that "[w]hile translation methods relate to whole texts, translation procedures are used for sentences and the smaller units of language".

The article argues that translation as a mediator between world languages works across power differentials when negotiating linguistic and cultural transactions among the language polarities of first and third worlds, the major and the minor, or the advanced and emerging cultures. Accordingly, the work of translation often lends itself to the "power-relations" strand of postcolonial studies, which has emerged as an interdisciplinary subject matter that investigates the hegemonic practices identified as "the ruling political, social, cultural, ideological and intellectual structures of a society" (Robinson, 1997: 13). This approach breaks away from colonial relations to investigate a more complex scenery of power hierarchy among nations across any timely interval whether historical or modern. Often termed as "power-relation studies", this approach is majorly concerned with the cultural exchange between dominant and less dominant groups, highlighting the underlying imbalance and the counter-efforts on the part of the latter to subvert the hegemony of the former and break free from subservience on political, social, and cultural levels (Robinson, 1997: 10–15).

Translation and cultural representation

Translation has emerged as a vital tool in steering cultural representation and redefining power relations. Translation is viewed as "a form of engagement as much as a form of writing"; it is an agent of resistance to "fetishizing of cultural objects and cultural constructs" (Tymoczko, 2000: 28–43). Translation practice is exposed to the linguistic and cultural systems of almost all global languages – an exposition that grants translation the privilege of influencing or shaping the hegemony and hierarchy of such languages. Hegemony, according to Gramsci (1998: 210), refers to the dominance or supremacy that the powerful group exercises on the less privileged to conquer them whether politically, economically, or even culturally or ideologically. Amidst such power dynamics, Bassnett and Trivedi (2002: 2) point out at the agency of translation:

> [t]ranslation is not an innocent, transparent activity but is highly charged with significance at every stage; it rarely, if ever, involves a relationship of equality between texts, authors or systems.

Meanwhile, Bassnett and Trivedi (2002: 16) argue that translation may collude with and "perpetuate" one front of power against the other. Likewise, Baker and Pérez-González (2011: 44) note that translators encounter areas of "radical inequality" in their pursuit of establishing channels of communication among cultures. They postulate that translators are in the habit of "asserting, questioning and sometimes forcefully resisting existing power structures" (2011: 44). Yet, they maintain that "translation does no resolve conflict and inequality by enabling dialogue but rather constitutes a space of tension and power struggle in its own right" (2011: 44). Translation deals with power structures through its selection of one particular approach to a given text rather than another; as approaches vary in their orientation towards the sending or the receiving culture, translation practice in turn sets the source and target texts in tension of power and dominance. This aligns with Tymoczko's (2000: 24) contention that the product of translation is "partisan: engaged and committed, either implicitly or explicitly". Accordingly, translations are imbued with ideological considerations and underlying political interventions targeting geopolitical and social outcomes.

Overview of Nida's translation theory

Nida's dichotomy of formal and dynamic equivalence has paved the way to a systematic linguistic analysis of translation. According to Munday (2001: 43), "Nida went a long way to [produce] a systematic analytical procedure for translators working with all kinds of text and he factored into the translation equation the receivers of the TT and their cultural expectations". Nida, (1964: 156–159) postulating that messages can differ in the extent to which they give priority to either the content or form of the text, introduces two different types of equivalence, each being applicable to certain situations: formal and dynamic equivalence.

Formal equivalence

In defining formal equivalence, Nida (1964) says "[f]ormal equivalence focuses attention on the message itself, in both form and content… One is concerned that the message in the receptor language should match as closely as possible the different elements in the source language".

According to Nida (1964), gloss translation is the most typical example of formal equivalence. This type of translation often involves footnotes to explain potential difficulties caused by the foreignness of the source language or its cultural background. The phrase "holy kiss", as exemplified by Nida (1964: 159), if occurs in a gloss translation, would be literally translated (an Arabic literal translation would be "القبلة المقدسة"), and followed by an explanatory footnote which reads that "this was a customary method of greeting in New Testament Times". Formal equivalence supports the supremacy of the source text through limiting the translator's interpretative interventions to the footnotes (Nida, 1964: 159). Therefore, it can be concluded that a formal equivalence translation intensifies the cultural hegemony of the original text, particularly when the original text is produced in a major language (such as English as a lingua franca).

Dynamic equivalence

A dynamic translation lessens the intensity of the source cultural hegemony through its reliance on receptor- oriented strategies. As Nida (1964: 159) perceives, dynamic equivalence complies with the principle of "naturalness of expression". Nida holds that a dynamic translation aims at achieving "the closest natural equivalent to the source language message" (1964: 166). Here, naturalness is achieved at the level of grammar, lexicon and cultural references and the target language is not supposed to show any interreference from the source language and aspects of "foreignness" are kept at a minimum (1964: 167). For instance, a dynamic translation of the phrase "greet someone with a holy kiss" would read "give one another a hearty handshake all around" (Nida, 1964: 160) or in Arabic would be "صافحه مصافحة حارة". In a dynamically translated text, readers are handed an intelligible text that flows in a natural, familiarized manner to the target reader, and one that keeps its translator invisible. Dynamic translation, which weighs the receptor's response over fidelity to the source, foregrounding natural target forms over "forms that may be traditionally more prestigious" (Nida & Taber, 1969: 14), allows the target language to counter the dominance of the culture sourcing the information. In this respect, the next section will illustrate, by the means of two example translations, how the supremacy of the source text/culture can be highlighted in formal equivalence and toned down in dynamic equivalence.

Application

This section presents the source text of the BCG matrix, which is a marketing model generally used to analyse a company's portfolio (including products and services) in order to make investment decisions. The matrix is intended to direct companies about which products are likely to generate profit or loss. This marketing model is composed of four categories: stars, question marks, cash cow, and dog (See Figure 1).

Source text of the BCG matrix

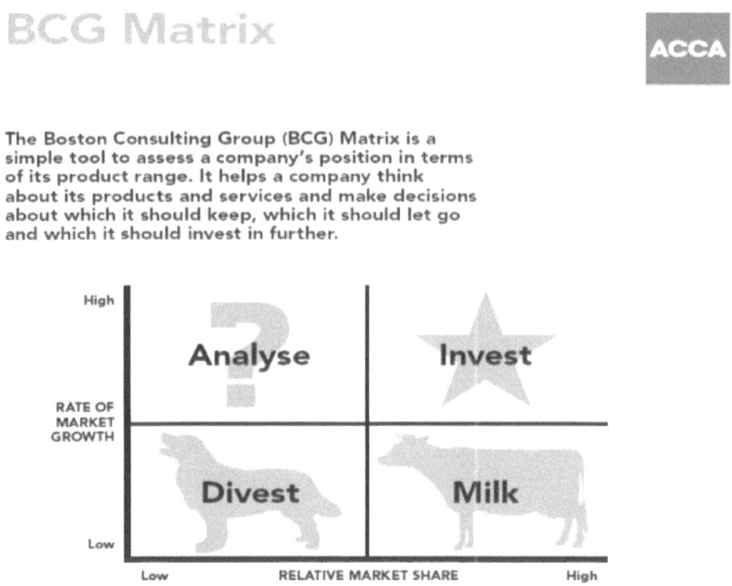

Question Marks

Question marks are products that grow rapidly and as a result consume large amounts of cash, but because they have low market shares they don't generate much cash. The result is a large net cash consumption. A question mark has the potential to gain market share and become a star, and eventually a cash cow when the market growth slows. If it doesn't become a market leader it will become a dog when market growth declines. Question marks need to be analysed carefully to determine if they are worth the investment required to grow market share.

Dogs

Dogs have a low market share and a low growth rate and neither generate nor consume a large amount of cash. However, dogs are cash traps because of the money tied up in a business that has little potential. Such businesses are candidates for divestiture.

Stars

Stars generate large sums of cash because of their strong relative market share, but also consume large amounts of cash because of their high growth rate. So the cash being spent and brought in approximately nets out. If a star can maintain its large market share it will become a cash cow when the market growth rate declines.

Cash Cows

As leaders in a mature market, cash cows exhibit a return on assets that is greater than the market growth rate – so they generate more cash than they consume. These units should be 'milked' extracting the profits and investing as little as possible. They provide the cash required to turn question marks into market leaders.

Figure 1. Source text of the BCG matrix (ACCA, n.d.)

Formal equivalence translation

This section provides a translation of the BCG matrix into Arabic following the approach of formal equivalence.

مصفوفة مجموعة بوسطن الاستشارية (BCG)

مصفوفة مجموعة بوسطن الاستشارية هي أداة مبسطة لتقييم وضع الشركة من حيث نطاق منتجاتها. وهي تساعد الشركة على التفكير في المنتجات والخدمات التي تقدمها واتخاذ قرارات بشأن تلك التي ينبغي الاحتفاظ بها وتلك التي ينبغي أن تتخلى عنها وتلك التي ينبغي أن تستثمر فيها أكثر.

Figure 2. Formal equivalence translation (Image is adapted from Professional Academy, 2024)

علامات الاستفهام Question Marks

علامات الاستفهام تشير إلى المنتجات التي تنمو بسرعة وكنتيجة لذلك تستنفد كميات كبيرة من النقدية، ولكن نظرًا لأنها تمتلك حصص سوقية منخفضة، فهي لا تدر الكثير من النقدية. النتيجة هي استنفاد كبير لصافي النقدية. علامة الاستفهام لديها إمكانية لكسب حصة سوقية وأن تصبح نجمة وأخيرًا بقرة حلوب عند تباطؤ النمو السوقي. إذا لم تصبح رائدة للسوق، ستصبح كلبا عندما ينخفض النمو السوقي. علامات الاستفهام تحتاج إلى تحليلها بعناية لتحديد إذا كانت تستحق الاستثمار المطلوب لنمو الحصة السوقية.

الكلاب Dogs

الكلاب لديها حصة سوقية منخفضة ومعدل نمو منخفض وهي لا تدر ولا تستنفد كمية كبيرة من النقدية. ومع ذلك، الكلاب تمثل مصائد للنقدية نظرًا لأن الأموال مرتبطة بعمل ذات إمكانية ضعيفة. وهذه الأعمال تكون مرشحة للتخارج.

النجوم Stars

النجوم تدر مبالغ كبيرة من النقدية بسبب حصتها السوقية القوية نسبيًا، لكن تستنفد أيضًا كميات كبيرة من النقدية بسبب معدل نموها المرتفع. ولذلك فإن النقدية التي تُنفق وتُحصل لا تُسجل مكسب صافي تقريبًا. وإذا نجحت النجمة في الإبقاء على حصتها السوقية الكبيرة، ستصبح بقرة حلوب عندما ينخفض معدل النمو السوقي.

الأبقار الحلوب Cash Cows

باعتبارها رواد في السوق الناضج، تقدم الأبقار الحلوب عائد على الأصول أكبر من معدل النمو السوقي- ولذلك فهي تدر نقدية أكبر مما تستنفدها. وهذه الوحدات ينبغي أن "تُحلب" لاستخلاص الأرباح والاستثمار بأقل قدر ممكن. وهي تُوفر النقدية المطلوبة لتحويل علامات الاستفهام إلى رواد للسوق.

Dynamic equivalence translation

This section provides a translation of the BCG matrix into Arabic following the approach of dynamic equivalence.

نموذج مجموعة بوسطن

تقدم مصفوفة مجموعة بوسطن الاستشارية نموذجًا مبسطًا لتقييم وضع الشركة من حيث محفظة منتجاتها. ومن خلال هذه المصفوفة، تستطيع الشركات دراسة المنتجات والخدمات التي تقدمها كي تقرر السياسة التي ستتبعها بشأن كل منها والتي تتفاوت بين الاحتفاظ أو التخارج أو ضخ مزيدًا من الاستثمارات.

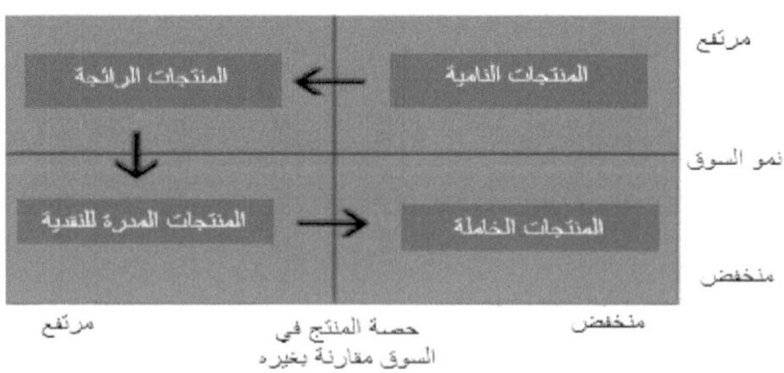

Figure 3. Dynamic equivalence translation (Image is adapted from Marketing Teacher, n.d.)

المنتجات النامية

يقصد بها المنتجات التي تتسم بالنمو السريع بما يجعلها تستنفد مبالغ نقدية كبيرة، إلا أنها لا تعد مصدرًا كبيرًا للنقدية نظرًا لانخفاض حصتها في السوق، وبالتالي ينتج عنها نضوبًا في بند صافي النقدية، وتحمل المنتجات النامية إمكانات للتطور إلى منتجات رائجة عند استحواذها على حصة في السوق، وبنهاية المطاف تصبح منتجات مدرة للنقدية عند تباطؤ نموها في السوق، غير أنها قد تتراجع إلى منتجات خاملة مع انخفاض معدل نموها في السوق حال إخفاقها في الوصول إلى مكانة رائدة، ولذا لابد من تحليل المنتجات النامية بدقة لتحديد جدوى الاستثمار فيها من عدمه دعمًا لنمو حصتها في السوق.

المنتجات الخاملة

هي المنتجات التي تنخفض حصتها في السوق ومعدل نموها؛ وبالتالي فهي لا تدر ولا تستنفد مبالغ نقدية كبيرة، إلا أنها تؤثر سلبًا على الرصيد النقدي الذي يوجه مبلغًا منه إلى أنشطة عمل محدودة الإمكانات وبالتالي فهي مرجحة للتخارج.

المنتجات الرائجة

يقصد بها المنتجات التي تدر مبالغ نقدية كبيرة نظرًا لارتفاع حصتها في السوق مقارنة بغيرها من المنتجات، غير أنها تستنفد قدرًا كبيرًا من الرصيد النقدي بسبب ارتفاع معدل نموها، ولذلك تتساوى نفقات هذه المنتجات مع إيراداتها تقريبًا بدون ربح. ويمكن للمنتجات الرائجة من خلال احتفاظها بحصة كبيرة في السوق أن تصبح مدرة للنقدية مع انخفاض معدل نموها بالسوق.

المنتجات المدرة للنقدية

تشير إلى المنتجات التي تحقق عائدًا على الأصول يفوق معدل النمو في السوق، حيث تحتل مركزًا تنافسيًا قويًا بالسوق الناضجة؛ وبالتالي فإن حجم النقدية الذي تدره يتجاوز القدر المستنفد، ولذا ينبغي استغلال هذه المنتجات لتحقيق أكبر قدر من الأرباح مع تقليل الاستثمار فيها قدر الإمكان، كما يمكن من خلالها توفير النقدية اللازمة لتطوير المنتجات النامية لتصبح رائدة للسوق.

Analysis

The study implies that marketing is one of the disciplines where translation can play a role in backing or curtailing the dominance of the source text and its cultural hegemony. Since marketing is a fully-fledged field in the Western world as opposed to Eastern countries, its translation might be immersed in the source background and thus suggesting its dominance. The BCG matrix provides a model of marketing that attests to BCG exclusivity by relying on emotive or expressive language. According to Macagno and Walton (2014: 5), emotive language is a persuasive mode that draws on the use of catchy words that capture the recipient's attention by conveying either positive or negative connotations. The same persuasive effect is tangible in Reiss's expressive text type which emulates creative aesthetic composition (Reiss, 2000: 163). The BCG matrix builds its marketing theory on key emotive terms including "Question Marks", "Dogs", "Stars" and "Cash Cows", which refer to a classification of products.

Such terms represent culture-specific words because when translated into another language, their meaning would be "totally unknown in the target culture" (Baker, 1992: 29), causing confusion to the receptor who is unfamiliar with the BCG matrix.

Rendering the BCG matrix into Arabic highlights the cultural engaged function of translation because the mechanisms of formal and dynamic equivalence can correspond to the metaphors of inferiority or cannibalism, respectively. While the former retains the emotive and expressive function of the source text, the latter adopts an informative textual function as resistance to the source cultural constructs. The choice to translate the above terms formally to their closest Arabic equivalents (علامات الاستفهام، الكلاب، النجوم، الأبقار الحلوب) sets the recipients in the source environment implying the dominance of the culture from which this marketing theory has emerged. Here, formal equivalence maintains the expressive and emotive force of the source text by adhering to the source lexis. Conversely, dynamic equivalence leaves the target reader at ease without being alerted of the cultural hegemony of the source model. The dynamic adaptation of these terms uses plain informative labels in Arabic as follows:

(المنتجات النامية، المنتجات الخاملة، المنتجات الرائجة، المنتجات المدرة للنقدية)

(Back translation: 'growing products', 'dormant' products, 'resilient products', 'cash generating products').

Dynamic equivalence produces an informative function defined by Reiss (1977/1989: 108) as "plain communication of facts" in logical form. The procedure used in these dynamic equivalence translations is situational equivalence in Vinay and Darbelnet's typology (1958/1995: 38), as it involves an act of changing the semantics of the SL term and expressing it in different lexical items since the literal rending could be unidiomatic in the TL. The equivalence procedure involved an act of lexical substitution, which stands for editing of the TT to make sure that it sounds natural. The dynamic equivalence approach entailed changing the source content so that the target text would convey a natural message without burdening the Arabic reader with the English emotive referents, hence questioning the hegemony of the source model. Therefore, the translational approach engages in shaping power structure either by enabling the target culture resistance or by empowering the source to claim dominance.

Another area where the translation can celebrate the source hegemony is in producing or deviating from a sort of "third code" that is defined by Frawley as a distinct way of expression that compromises the lexical styles of the source and target languages (Frawley, 2000: 257). It can be noted that formal equivalence compromises the source and target linguistic patterns in a third code as opposed to a natural code in the dynamic equivalence translation. Third code is evident in preserving the lexical norms of the source language in the formal-equivalence translation. An example is the translation of "cash traps" as "مصائد للنقدية" which represents a literal rendering or what is defined by Vinay and Darbelnet (1958/1995: 33) as a word-for-word translation. Such translation constitutes a third code because it would not convey a natural collocation to the Arab reader. In the dynamic translation, the term is rendered as "تؤثر سلبًا على الرصيد النقدي" (back translation: negatively impacting the cash balance), employing Vinay and Darbelnet's (1958/1995: 38) procedure of equivalence which accounts for explaining the same situation using a completely different phrase. Likewise, formal equivalence exhibits a third code in rendering the sentence "These units should be 'milked' extracting the profits" as "هذه الوحدات ينبغي أن تُحلب لاستخلاص الأرباح" offering a literal translation of the verb "milked" which would be received by the Arab receptor as odd despite it is provided under the category of cash cows "الأبقار الحلوب". The dynamic translation of the same sentence reads: "ينبغي استغلال هذه المنتجات لتحقيق أكبر قدر من الأرباح" (back translation: such products should be exploited to achieve the maximum profitability). This dynamic translation is based on the above-mentioned equivalence procedure as it communicates the meaning of the verb "milk" without adhering to the source lexical style. Hence, it is evident that formal equivalence sticks to the source content resulting in a third code, whereas dynamic equivalence concentrates on generating a natural code in the target text.

The focus on structural and graphic consistency in the formal translation gives validity to the source language, while in dynamic equivalence the structure and graphics are adapted to fulfill a natural code in the target language. In rendering the statement "make decisions about which it should keep, which it should let go and which it should invest in further"

"اتخاذ قرارات بشأن تلك التي ينبغي الاحتفاظ بها، وتلك التي ينبغي أن تتخلى عنها، وتلك التي ينبغي أن تستثمر فيها أكثر" as, the translation attempts to mirror the original structure as much as possible. On the other hand, dynamic equivalence rephrased the statement differently as "تقرر السياسة التي ستتبعها بشأن كل منها والتي تتفاوت بين الاحتفاظ بها، أو التخارج، أو ضخ مزيدًا من الاستثمارات" (back translation: decide on the policy to follow about each of them, which may vary between keeping, divesting or pumping more investments) – the procedure of transposition in Vinay and Darbelnet's (1958/1995: 36), or changing the word class (from verb phrase to gerund form) is employed to enhance naturalness in the target text. Fidelity to the source elements is manifested in retaining the same graphic patterns (image of the dog, cow, etc.) in the formal equivalence translation. However, the dynamic equivalence version omits the source graphic patterns, compensating them with the use of arrows to explain the lifecycle of products as defined by the content. Such process draws on Vinay and Darbelnet's (1958/1995: 169) procedure of gains and losses, which refers to a way of compensation whereby some information or stylistic effect are compensated by other means. In sum, the orientations of formal equivalence stem from faithfulness to the source, while those of dynamic equivalence intend to naturalize the target text to meet the receptors' expectations.

Discussion

Translation mediates linguistic and cultural flow from one language into another. This act of mediation is not always arbitrary; rather it can sometimes be subtly oriented towards asserting or downplaying the power and authority of a certain culture. In contexts of power inequality between the sending and receiving cultures, translation can approach an issue with either with a scheme of aggrandizing or devouring its force. Within this power struggle, a formal translation would function as validation of the dominance of the source language, admitting the inferiority of the target text to the original. Adversely, a dynamic translation transforms the power relationship between a text and its translation to a new level in which the target culture is not ancillary to the source; instead, it "interacts with the source culture, drawing upon it for nourishment but creating something new" (Bassnett, 1993: 154). Hence, formal equivalence draws on the metaphor of the translator as a slave, whereas dynamic equivalence is an approach that classifies the translation as an act of cannibalism.

Strict adherence and fidelity to the foreign pattern of the source in a formal equivalence translation reduces the translation to an inferior position as to its original text when the power legitimacy of the source is questioned in the translation process. Bassnett (1993: 147) notes that the view of translation as a manifestation of inferiority and of the translator as "the servant of the source text" dates back to the nineteenth century era of colonization. She further elaborates "[i]mplicit in this metaphor is the idea of dominance of the source text author over the subservient target text". Similarly, Niranjana (1992) argues that colonialism offers a typical reflection of the poetics of hegemony and dialectical representation of the powerful force and the other, by the means of translation. Niranjana (1992: 2) notes that the hegemonic group establishes itself as the dominant ideology and the legitimate source of knowledge and in such context "translation both shapes and takes shape within the asymmetrical relations of power that operate under colonialism". To contextualize the inferiority of the translation to its original, Bassnett and Trivedi (2002) question the relationship between translation and colonialism. During the early colonial period, as Bassnett and Trivedi (2002: 4) highlight:

> Europe was regarded as the great Original, the starting point, and the colonies were therefore copies, or 'translations' of Europe, which they were supposed to duplicate. Moreover, being copies, translations were evaluated as less than originals.

At this period, European works were regarded as the canon and the superlative, while their translation was seen as "something that diminished the greater original" (Bassnett & Trivedi, 2002: 3–4). There was an inherent dogma that translation cannot be void of gaps, which entails superiority of the original. The metaphor assigned to translation at that time was that of a copy or a portrait that lacks the essence of the original (Maybin & Swann, 2010: 279). Hence, a formal translation that is keenly oriented towards matching the form and content of the source as closely as possible implies the dominance of the source language in its pursuit to copy the original.

On the contrary, dynamic equivalence triggers the translation to challenge the dominance of the source language by adapting its linguistic and cultural elements to meet the conventions of the target background. A dynamic translation fulfills the standard laid down by Benjamin (2012) as being “an after-life, a survival, a continuation through renascence, and not as a copy” (Bassnett 1993: 153) Given its appropriation of the source text for achieving a natural effect on the receiver, dynamic equivalence conforms to what Bassnett and Trivedi (2002: 52) refer to as the cannibalistic metaphor of translation developed by postcolonial theorists. According to Bassnett (1993: 153), Oswald de Andrade’s Manifesto Antropófago introduced the metaphor of cannibalism to suggest “a new attitude towards cultural relationships with hegemonic powers”. It is an attitude where the receiving culture does not copy the source; it devours the foreign input, processes and reproduces it in a natural form that would appeal to its receptors. Commenting on the cannibalistic theory to translation, Else Vieira (1994: 72) writes:

> in the cannibalistic philosophy, translation becomes a two-way flow, the very terminology ‘source’ and ‘target’ becomes depleted. By the same token, the power relation between source and target, superior/inferior ceases to exist.

Thus, the dynamic equivalence that authorizes the translator to adapt the target text to the expectations of its audience strikes balance in terms of power between the sending and receiving cultures.

Insights into translation pedagogy

The theoretical implications of the findings from the two translation versions suggest pedagogical insights with regard to the teaching practices of translation. Although this study focuses on discursive linguistic features and their ideological slants, the findings may well have a bearing on the dynamics of building translation competency in an interactive translation learning environment. The data suggest that learning translation in the classroom can be achieved through integrating three criteria for learning: flipped, deep, and experiential. Generally, in the literature on pedagogy, the term “flipped learning” tends to be used to refer to a form of knowledge acquisition whereby students review the learning material before the class to “acquire knowledge” and be prepared to “use the classroom time to practice and apply concepts and ideas through interaction with peers and teachers" (Advance HE, 2018). However, the "flipped approach" can be tailored in its broadest sense of "flipping" to support the notion that there is no single correct way to translate, and that translators often encounter an array of linguistic choices; thus, the conventional notion of "the best translation" can be inverted and substituted by the competency to make informed translation decisions. This approach strengthens the idea that we should not teach translators the right way to translate but allow translators to develop critical thinking through discussions and activities that allow the learner to employ their analytical skills and explore independent thinking.

The flipped approach has a number of attractive features. A major advantage of the flipped approach is that it fosters the characteristics of what Biggs and Tang (2011: 26) refer to conceptually as "deep learning" given its aim to "understand the big picture" and deepen understanding through promoting discussion and problem-solving skills. In principle, the "deep approach" abandons short-cut knowledge acquisition by moving in favor of an in-depth understanding (Biggs & Tang, 2011: 26). This method of knowledge acquisition is one of the more practical ways of learning as it opts for providing the building blocks or explaining the general steps, thereby allowing the learner to search independently for the required information. It avoids the problem of the "surface approach" which is associated with learning practices that rely primarily on memorizing information rather than understanding (Biggs & Tang, 2011: 24). Moreover, flipped learning is considered one of the most practical ways of the "student-centered model of teaching" (Biggs & Tang, 2011: 20), as the delivery strategy takes the form of a recap presentation, discussion and formative feedback following activities completed by students. Accordingly, learners can acquire "troublesome knowledge" and benefit from "formative feedback" (i.e., feedback for learning rather than grading) in a challenging, engaging and inspiring environment (Norton, 2009: 137; Perkins, 2006: 37).

In most cases, translation pedagogy strives to mark an intersection between what Becher and Trowler (2001: 186) refer to as soft pure and hard-applied knowledge, i.e., theory and practice. The aim is to achieve "high- quality learning outcomes" which feature a transformational learning experience that can be utilized "in other and new contexts" (Prosser & Trigwell, 1999: 108). In this regard, Kolb's experiential learning cycle can be usefully employed to map out the learning process and its intended outcomes (Kurt, 2022), as illustrated by Figure 4 below.

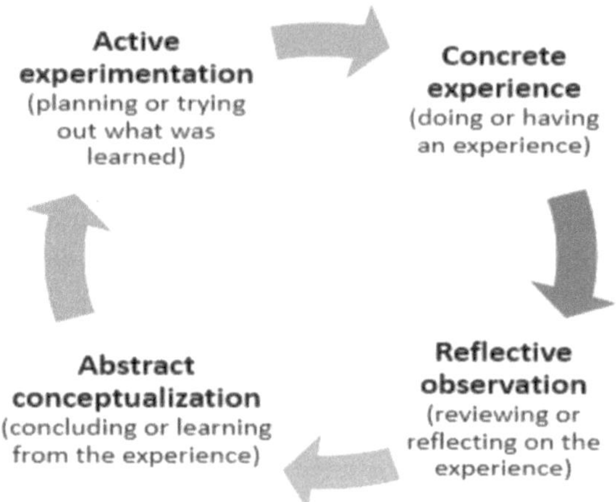

Figure 4. Kolb's experiential learning cycle (Kurt, 2022)

Kolb's experiential learning theory follows a four-stage cycle, which transforms experience into knowledge. The first stage of the learning process aims to build concrete experience by engaging in a task or having hands-on experience (Kurt, 2022). This reflects an experiential learning, which builds upon "having an experience, or 'doing', but also reflecting, processing, thinking and furthering understanding, and usually 'improvement' the next time something is encountered or done" (Norton, 2009: 16). The second stage is a reflective observation where learners can practice self-reflection or engage in discussions with their peers. The third stage of abstract conceptualization is based on interpreting their experience to draw conclusions. In the final stage of active experimentation, learners should be able to employ their acquired knowledge to new experiences (Kurt, 2022).

Applying Kolb's learning theory to translation pedagogy requires translators to actively engage in translation tasks. Teaching translation should then feature provoking and reflective discussions about the critical approaches that interpret translation choices and grapple with the way informed decisions are carefully made with a view to interacting with the surrounding political and cultural context. When practicing translation in class, cooperative/group work can be fruitful and rewarding in identifying appropriate translation methodologies and generating competent translations, through discussions and exchanging opinions about suitable expressions and ways of achieving original composition that would sound more natural to the audience, thus forming and modifying conclusions. Equally important is asking students to write a reflective essay on their translations in order to ensure that they grasp the rationale behind their translation decisions, which are generally held to be non-random unless driven by linguistic discrepancy – thus reaching general statements that can be usefully applied to new situations.

In fact, achieving the learning outcomes of Kolb's cycle lends itself to constructive alignment with the following three assessment strategies: Assessment AS learning, Assessment FOR learning, Assessment OF learning. *Concrete experience* may be evaluated through the strategy of *assessment AS learning*, which refers to the activities and assignments used to promote understanding and engage students in the learning process (National Forum, 2016). This strategy represents a *self-assessment*, which Boud and Falchikov (1989: 529) define as "the involvement of learners in making judgments about their achievements and the outcomes of their learning". This self-assessment establishes a "student-centered model of teaching" that focuses on "what *students* do" (Biggs & Tang, 2011: 20), by enabling them to contemplate upon their concrete experience and gauge their learning outcome against the defined criteria. This also promotes the academic integrity principle to foster "self-regulated learners" (National Forum, 2017). *Reflective observation* will capture the strategy of *assessment FOR learning,* which is a type of assessment for "giving feedback on teaching and student learning" (National Forum, 2016). Finally, *abstract conceptualization* and *active experimentation* will be cornerstone for the summative *assessment OF learning*, i.e., "testing what has been learned" (Norton, 2009: 134) through assignments that promote the academic integrity principles of maintaining "diverse" albeit integrated assessment methods (National Forum, 2017).

Conclusion

The aim of the present research is to examine the agency of translation in business communication and how different translation approaches can have cultural implications. In this investigation, the article has presented two translations of the Boston Consulting Group (BCG) Matrix, one based on formal equivalence and the other on dynamic equivalence. In translating the BCG Matrix from English into Arabic, formal equivalence lies emphasis on the source dominance through restoring the culture-specific and syntactic elements of the source text and often results in a third code or distinct linguistic features that result from interlingual transfer. Dynamic equivalence, on the contrary, tailors the content and form of the source to the Arab receptor's cultural background and therefore challenging the source hegemony.

Accordingly, translation is endowed with the ability to influence power relations among the cultures it mediates. In contexts where the West holds the distinction of being the primary source of advancement, translation can celebrate their pioneering achievements through adopting formal equivalence to bring to the reader's attention the foreign patterns and imply dominance of the source culture. Yet, it can adapt the foreign knowledge to the receptor's expectations to mitigate the hegemony of the sending culture and promote a multicultural model of knowledge. In the latter approach, "the receiving culture will interpenetrate and transform the original one" (Bassnett, 1993: 155), thereby resisting cultural hegemony and establishing a balanced cultural structure. As such, "translation is not just 'a window opened on another world'... Rather, translation is a channel opened" (Bassnett, 1993: 159) through which cultures can interact for integration, resistance, or any other purpose. The findings, thus, provide an opportunity to advance our knowledge of translation pedagogy based on a three-tiered conceptual theoretical framework that explores the association between translation competency and the principles of flipped, deep and experiential learning.

References

ACCA Global. (n.d.). http://www.accaglobal.com/content/dam/acca/gb/graduates/boston_consulting.pdf

Advance HE. (2018). Flipped learning. https:// www.adva nce- he.ac.uk/ knowledge-hub/flipped-learning-0.

Baker M. & Pérez- González, L. (2011). *Translation and interpreting from: The Routledge Handbook of Applied Linguistics*. Routledge.

Baker, M. (1992). *In other words a coursebook on translation*. Routledge.

Bassnett, S. (1993). *Comparative literature: A critical introduction*. Blackwell.

Bassnett, S. & Trivedi, H. (2002). *Post- colonial translation theory and practice*. Routledge.

Becher, T. & Trowler, P. (2001). *Academic tribes and territories: Intellectual enquiry and the culture of disciplines* (2nd ed.). The Society for Research into Higher Education & Open University Press.

Benjamin, W. (2012). The task of the translator: An introduction to the translation of Baudelaire's tableaux parisiens. Translated by H. Zohn. In L. Venuti (Ed.), *The translation studies reader* (pp. 15–25). Routledge.

Biggs, J. & Tang, C. (2011). *Teaching for quality learning at university* (4th ed.). Open University Press.

Boud, D. & Falchikov, N. (1989). Quantitative studies of student self-assessment and peer assessment. *Higher Education,* 18(5): 529–49.

Frawley, W. (2000). Prolegomenon to a theory of translation. In L. Venuti (Ed.), *The translation studies reader* (pp. 250–263). Routledge Taylor & Francis Group.

Gramsci, A. (1998). Hegemony, intellectuals and the state. In J. Storey (Ed.), *Cultural theory and popular culture: A reader* (pp. 210–216). Prentice Hall.

Kolb, D. A. (1984). *Experiential learning: Experience as the source of learning and development*. Prentice Hall.

Kurt, S. (2022, September 25). Kolb's experiential learning theory & learning styles. *Educational Technology Consulting Services*. https:// educationaltechnology.net/kolbs-experiential-learning-theory-learning-styles/.

Macagno, F. & Walton, D. (2014). *Emotive language in argumentation*. Cambridge University Press.

Marketing Teacher (n.d.) Boston Matrix. https://www.marketingteacher.com/boston-matrix/

Maybin, J. & Swann, J. (2010). *The Routledge companion to English language studies*. Routledge.

Merriam-Webster. (2018). *What is the difference between acculturation, assimilation, and amalgamation?* https://www.merriam-webster.com/dictionary/amalgamation.

Munday, J. (2001). *Introducing translation studies: Theories and applications*. Routledge.

National Forum for the Enhancement of Teaching and Learning in Higher Education. (2016). *Enhancement theme: Assessment OF, FOR and AS learning: students as partners in assessment.* https://www.teachingandlearning.ie/publication/students-as-partners

National Forum for the Enhancement of Teaching and Learning in Higher Education. (2017). *Assessment OF/FOR/AS learning enhancement theme 2016–18.* https://www.teachingandlearning.ie/wp-content/uploads/NF-2017-Assessment-OFFORAS-Learning-Enhancement-Theme-2016-18.pdf

Newmark, P. (1988). *A textbook of translation*. Prentice-Hall International.

Nida, E. & Taber, C. (1969). *The theory and practice of translation.* E.J. Brill.

Nida, E. A. (1964). *Toward a science of translating*. Leiden: E.J. Brill.

Niranjana, T. (1992). *Siting translation history, post-structuralism, and the colonial context.* University of California Press.

Norton, L. (2009). Assessing student learning. In H. Fry, S. Ketteridge & S. Marshall (Eds.), *A handbook for teaching and learning in higher education* (3rd ed., pp. 132–149). Routledge.

Perkins, D. (2006). Constructivism and troublesome knowledge. In J. Meyer & R. Land (Eds.), *Overcoming barriers to student understanding: Threshold concepts and troublesome knowledge* (pp. 33–47). Routledge.

Professional Academy (2024) Marketing theories – Boston consulting group matrix. https://www.professionalacademy.com/blogs/marketing-theories-boston-consulting-group-matrix/

Prosser, M. & Trigwell, K. (1999). *Understanding learning and teaching. The experience in higher education.* Society for Research into Higher Education and the Open University Press.

Reiss, K. (1977/1989). Text types, translation types and translation assessment. Translated by A. Chesterman. In A. Chesterman (Ed.), *Readings in translation theory* (pp. 105–15). Oy Finn Lectura Ab.

Reiss, K. (2000). Type, kind and individuality of text: Decision making in translation. Translated by S. Kitron. In L. Venuti (Ed.), *The translation studies reader* (pp. 160–171). Routledge Taylor & Francis Group.

Robinson, D. (1997). *Translation and empire: Postcolonial theories explained.* St. Jerome Publishing.

Tymoczko, M. (2000). Translation and political engagement. *The Translator,* 6(1): 23–47.

Vieira, E. (1994). A postmodern translational aesthetics in Brazil. In M. Snell-Hornby, K. Kaindl & F. Pöchhacker (Eds.), *Translation studies: An interdiscipline* (pp. 65–72). John Benjamins.

Vinay, J. & Darbelnet, J. (1995). *Comparative stylistics of French and English: A methodology for translation.* Translated and edited by J. C. Sager & M. J. Hamel. Amsterdam: John Benjamins. [Original French published 1958 as *Stylistique comparee du francais et de l'anglais: Methode de traduction*. Paris: Didier].

Julieta Amorebieta y Vera

3 Problemas de equivalencia e implicancias pedagógicas de la traducción de sociedades comerciales

It is well-known that the translation of "commercial", "economic" or "financial" texts takes place in contexts involving economic transactions or exchanges (Mayoral, 2007: 33) and it constitutes a branch of specialised translation in which texts belonging to different languages share such features as format and content. It should also be pointed out that certain aspects of economic translation are closely related to legal translation and inseparable from it, as is the case of the translation of business documents. This brings into the picture the complex inequivalence problem between legal systems, which in turn highlights all terminological challenges that need solving. This article aims at analysing possible equivalences (or inequivalences) between business organizations in Argentina and England, any terminological problems implied and the implications all this may have on the teaching of specialized translation. To do this, different business forms from both jurisdictions will be described and analysed, taking advantage of comparative law resources, in an attempt to find equivalences and compare the terminology of the field. Finally, problems identified during legal and economic translation classes will be discussed, and solutions will be proposed based on the types of challenges observed.

Introducción

La traducción denominada "comercial", "económica" o "financiera" tiene lugar en contextos de intercambio o actividad económica y, debido a factores tales como la globalización y la necesidad de estandarización, los textos que se producen en las distintas lenguas muchas veces comparten tanto características de formato como aspectos de contenido (Mayoral, 2007: 33). Sin embargo, es importante destacar que existen ciertos aspectos de la traducción que, en lo sucesivo, denominaremos económica –si bien entendemos que las denominaciones varían según los aportes teóricos que se tomen (Gallego et al., 2016: 37)– que presentan estrechas conexiones con la traducción jurídica y son indisociables de ella, como es el caso de la traducción de documentos societarios.

La traducción jurídica, por sustanciarse entre distintos sistemas, en ocasiones pertenecientes a familias jurídicas diferentes, trae aparejada necesariamente la posibilidad de encontrarse con el complejo problema de la falta de equivalencias. Ello se percibe a primera vista a nivel terminológico; sin embargo, un análisis minucioso de la terminología muy probablemente lleve al traductor a concluir que las inequivalencias son más bien conceptuales. El nivel superficial de la lengua no hace más que poner de relieve las diferencias internas entre los sistemas jurídicos y los recursos que cada uno emplea para sortear los problemas que plantea la realidad.

Tanto es así que, tal como explica Socorro Trujillo (2016: 264), es fundamental que el traductor especializado cuente con conocimiento relativo a los géneros textuales, lo que algunos autores denominan competencia textual o de género (García Izquierdo, 2005). Es decir, debe conocer los esquemas conceptuales que se articulan en los textos. Estar familiarizado con la estructuración retórica prototípica y las normas que rigen los textos (tanto de origen como meta) constituye, así, uno de los niveles de conocimiento que proporcionan el andamiaje necesario para que el aprendiz de traducción logre, en definitiva, traducciones de calidad.

En esta misma línea, Alcalde Peñalver (2016: 284) plantea la gran importancia que tiene "la necesidad de contar con un profundo conocimiento del tema para poder afrontar con garantía de calidad los requisitos que se demandan en el mercado a la hora de contratar servicios de traducción financiera". Este postulado resulta, sin duda, relevante para todas las ramas de la traducción especializada. No obstante, en esta oportunidad nos interesa recalcar la relevancia que reviste el conocimiento extralingüístico en los textos en los que convergen la materia jurídica con la materia económica, por estar íntimamente ligado a la complejidad y al dinamismo que ellos presentan.

El derecho societario en Argentina

El derecho societario, denominación que rige para la República Argentina, es aquel que regula las relaciones contractuales de quienes participan de un negocio. Dado que el sistema jurídico argentino pertenece a la familia romano-germánica, nos encontramos con una rama del derecho altamente desarrollada y una gama de formas societarias sumamente tipificadas. En la actualidad las sociedades comerciales están reguladas por la Ley 19550 de 1972, con las modificaciones introducidas a partir de la sanción del Código Civil y Comercial de la Nación en 2015. Dicha ley tiene por objeto regular en un único cuerpo todos los tipos societarios pasibles de ser adoptados en el país, además de tutelar el interés general y proteger a los socios minoritarios, a los acreedores y a los terceros.

El Código Civil y Comercial de la Nación (2015) en su artículo 141 define a las personas jurídicas como "todos los entes a los cuales el ordenamiento jurídico les confiere aptitud para adquirir derechos y contraer obligaciones para el cumplimiento de su objeto y fines de su creación". Esto significa, entonces, que las sociedades comerciales son personas jurídicas o, en su antigua denominación, personas de existencia ideal. Como explica Nissen (2019: 4), la ley "limita la actuación de los sujetos colectivos a la celebración de todos los actos jurídicos que considere necesarios, pero siempre que tengan relación con el cumplimiento del objeto o el fin de su creación".

Vítolo (2016: 548), por su parte, agrega que la norma entiende por sociedad

> una *asociación* de dos o más personas –como principio general–, o una organización nacida de la declaración de voluntad unilateral de otro sujeto –con carácter excepcional–, que *en forma organizada* conforme a uno de los tipos previstos por la ley –o por fuera de ella, según el art. 21–, se obliga a *realizar aportes* –que es el acto de incorporación al grupo social mediante la provisión de elemento necesario para poder llevar adelante la función grupal, reuniéndose en un contexto limitado–, para *aplicarlos a la producción o intercambio de bienes y servicios* –propósito restringido– y *participando en los beneficios y soportando las perdidas* –cara y contracara, respectivamente, de las reglas de responsabilidad interna grupal–.

En esta oportunidad nos interesa tomar para nuestro análisis los tipos societarios más comunes recogidos por la norma, a saber: la sociedad colectiva, la sociedad en comandita simple, la sociedad en comandita por acciones, la sociedad de responsabilidad limitada y la sociedad anónima. Motiva esta selección la frecuencia con la que se constituyen este tipo de sociedades y el interés comparativo propio del campo de la traducción.

Las sociedades en Argentina, entonces, son sujetos de derecho; es decir, son susceptibles de adquirir derechos y obligaciones; y se constituyen y modifican por instrumento público o privado, el cual se inscribe en el Registro Público o Inspección General de Justicia, según la jurisdicción.

Las sociedades colectivas están regidas por el artículo 125 de la Ley 19550, en donde se establece que los socios tienen responsabilidad subsidiaria, ilimitada y solidaria. Al igual que las sociedades en comandita simple, las sociedades colectivas son sociedades de personas. Esto implica que las variaciones de socios generan cambios en el contrato social. La norma establece que es el contrato el que regula su régimen de administración; sin embargo, si este no lo hiciese, puede hacerlo cualquier socio indistintamente. Además, la ley establece la imposibilidad de los socios de competir con la sociedad.

Por su parte, el artículo 134 regula las sociedades en comandita simple. Estas formas societarias tienen la particularidad de contar con dos tipos de socios: socios comanditados y socios comanditarios. Los primeros tienen responsabilidad ilimitada y solidaria, mientras que los segundos responden únicamente con el capital que aportan. Esto, por tanto, imposibilita que los socios comanditarios participen de la administración so pena de convertirse en socios comanditados. Existe, asimismo, la posibilidad de que se designe un tercero para que lleve adelante la administración.

La sociedad en comandita por acciones comparte las características de la sociedad en comandita simple, pero está sujeta a las normas de la sociedad anónima, dado que su capital está dividido en acciones. En cuanto a la forma de gobierno, el órgano que representa la voluntad de la sociedad es la asamblea de accionistas, la cual está integrada por ambos tipos de socios. El control de la sociedad, por su parte, lo llevará a cabo la sindicatura, que estará a cargo de uno o más síndicos, según lo determinado por la asamblea de accionistas.

El artículo 146 de la ley regula las sociedades de responsabilidad limitada, las cuales se caracterizan principalmente por el hecho de que todos sus socios tienen responsabilidad limitada a la integración de las cuotas que suscriban o adquieren. El capital social, entonces, está dividido en cuotas de igual valor, las cuales deben suscribirse en su totalidad en el momento de la integración o constitución si los aportes fueran en especie; ahora bien, si los aportes son en dinero, puede integrarse un 25 por ciento inicialmente y luego el remanente dentro de un plazo de dos años. Las cuotas siempre son transmisibles libremente, salvo especificación en contrario en el contrato societario; sin embargo, la transmisión no puede prohibirse sino únicamente limitarse. Una cuestión interesante respecto de este tipo de sociedades es que presenta una restricción en cuanto a la cantidad de socios permitidos, puesto que solo pueden constituirse con hasta cincuenta socios, y el tipo de socios, puesto que únicamente habilita a las personas físicas a ser parte de este tipo de sociedad.

La ley además establece que la administración de la sociedad debe ser llevada a cabo por una gerencia, integrada por uno o más gerentes, quienes pueden ser socios o no y quienes cuentan con los mismos derechos y obligaciones que los directores de las sociedades anónimas. Los gerentes no pueden competir con la sociedad y son responsables individual o solidariamente, según lo que se establezca en el contrato. Además de este órgano, las sociedades de responsabilidad limitada pueden contar con un órgano de fiscalización, sindicatura o consejo de vigilancia, el cual se vuelve obligatorio si el capital alcanza los diez millones de pesos. En caso de no poseerlo, es responsabilidad de los socios ejercer la función de control. Para finalizar, las resoluciones que tomen este tipo de sociedades deben constar en actas y los libros deben conservarse durante tres años.

Otro tipo societario muy común en Argentina es el de la sociedad anónima, cuyo capital está representado por acciones. Esto genera que la responsabilidad de los socios esté limitada por las acciones suscriptas. Hasta la modificación del Código, las sociedades anónimas podían incluir dos o más personas de existencia visible, sin límite máximo. La nueva norma ha incorporado tanto la posibilidad de constituir sociedades anónimas unipersonales como la posibilidad de que sus socios sean tanto personas humanas como jurídicas.

Las sociedades por acciones tienen la particularidad de que deben constituirse por instrumento público y por acto único. Para ello deberán inscribirse los dos documentos constitutivos (el contrato y el estatuto) en el Registro correspondiente. El capital, dijimos, está dividido en acciones, las cuales deben ser de igual valor, expresado en pesos argentinos, pero pueden ser de diferente clase, lo que otorga distintos derechos. Las acciones son instrumentos financieros de libre transmisión, por lo que el estatuto societario puede limitar pero no prohibirla. Además de acciones, las sociedades anónimas pueden emitir bonos, tanto de goce como de participación.

En cuanto a la estructura societaria, se establecen tres órganos. El directorio es el órgano de administración de la sociedad y pueden estar formado por socios o por terceros. La función de representación está a cargo del presidente, lo que le permite a la sociedad vincularse jurídicamente con terceros. El directorio es el encargado de llevar a cabo la voluntad social, pero siempre es el presidente quien la expresa. El órgano de gobierno es la asamblea ordinaria o asamblea de accionistas, cuyos socios deben reunirse para deliberar. Los socios tendrán la facultad, además, de constituir asambleas extraordinarias. Por último, las sociedades anónimas pueden contar con un órgano de contralor o fiscalización, el cual será optativo, salvo para las empresas comprendidas por el artículo 299 de la ley.

El derecho societario en Inglaterra

En Inglaterra y Gales, puesto que ambos países conforman una misma jurisdicción, los distintos tipos societarios no se hallan recogidos en un único cuerpo legal, sino más bien en distintas leyes, dependiendo de la clase de sociedad de que se trate. Si nos centramos puramente en el aspecto terminológico, podemos agrupar estas figuras en dos grandes grupos: *partnerships* y *companies*. Sin embargo, no todas las sociedades denominadas *partnerships* están regidas por la misma ley, ni todas las sociedades incluidas en la denominada *Companies Act* comparten idénticas características. Es por ello que creemos conveniente hacer un repaso por las normas y las características que para ellas allí se establecen.

En primer lugar, cabe aclarar que existen tres leyes diferentes para las denominadas *partnerships*: *the Partnership Act 1890, the Limited Partnerships Act 1907* y *the Limited Liability Partnerships Act 2000*. La primera de estas leyes establece las disposiciones que regulan las sociedades conocidas como *standard, ordinary* o *general partnerships*. Al igual que las *limited partnerships* y las *limited liability partnerships*, las *standard partnerships* pueden conformarse con un mínimo de dos socios y siempre persiguen fines de lucro.

En el caso de las *standard partnerships*, todos los socios, por ser dueños de la sociedad, tienen la responsabilidad conjunta de la dirección de la empresa, tienen responsabilidad ilimitada y solidaria frente a las deudas o pérdidas de la sociedad, y pueden optar por celebrar un contrato escrito para la creación de la sociedad o no. Si no lo hiciesen, la ley establece que todos los socios tienen derecho a recibir ganancias en idéntica proporción y deben afrontar las pérdidas de la misma manera. Además, la totalidad de los socios debe involucrarse en la administración de la sociedad y no pueden admitirse nuevos socios sin su consentimiento. Por último, solo puede modificarse el contrato con el consentimiento expreso de todos los socios y no puede desvincularse a ningún socio por mayoría de votos a menos que se hayan acordado dichas facultades con anterioridad. Además, la sociedad se extingue por el fallecimiento o la quiebra de alguno de los socios, por decisión judicial, por acuerdo de las partes o por vencimiento del plazo estipulado.

Por su parte, la ley denominada *Limited Partnerships Act 1907* establece que, en este tipo de sociedades, se limita la cantidad de socios a un máximo de veinte, de los cuales al menos uno debe responder con todo su patrimonio ante las deudas, es decir, tiene responsabilidad ilimitada. Esto lo hace responsable de la administración de la sociedad, mientras que los demás socios solo tienen responsabilidad limitada a los aportes de capital que hayan realizado. Es por ello que si se involucran en actos de administración pierden el beneficio y responden con todo su patrimonio ante las pérdidas que ocurriesen. Este tipo de sociedad, a diferencia de la anterior, no se extingue por fallecimiento. Es decir, ya no es una sociedad de personas.

Las disposiciones de la *Limited Liability Partnerships Act 2000* posibilitan una tercera estructura societaria como similar denominación, pero que se considera un *body corporate*, al igual que las *companies*. Así, todos los socios de las *limited liability partnerships* gozan del beneficio de la responsabilidad limitada. Gran parte de las regulaciones que afectan este tipo societario están comprendidas en las normas que rigen otro tipo societario, las *companies,* dado que ambas constituyen personas jurídicas independientes de sus socios. Las *limited liability partnerships* se extinguen por acuerdo de las partes, mediante notificación expresa, y no exigen una cantidad máxima de socios. Dado que combina características de las *partnerships* y de las *companies*, los requisitos para la constitución de la sociedad son más exigentes. Por ejemplo, es obligación registrar el contrato societario o documento constitutivo en la autoridad pertinente (*Registrar of Companies*).

Por otra parte, en Inglaterra y Gales existe un cuarto tipo societario denominado *company*. Estas pueden ser públicas o privadas, en relación con la cotización en bolsa, y sus socios pueden tener responsabilidad ilimitada, limitada por las acciones que hayan suscripto o limitada por la garantía que hayan ofrecido. Además, al igual que lo que sucede con las *limited liability partnerships*, los socios pueden ser tanto personas humanas como jurídicas.

Las sociedades denominadas *companies*, entonces, pueden ofrecen varias opciones a su socio o socios: *public company limited by shares, private company limited by shares, private company limited by guarantee* o *private unlimited company*. Las sociedades en las que la responsabilidad de los socios está limitada a las acciones suscriptas pueden ser tanto públicas como privadas. Esto determina simplemente si las acciones cotizan en bolsa o no. Las sociedades cuyos socios tienen responsabilidad limitada por la garantía ofrecida en el acto de constitución generalmente son las más elegidas para la creación de instituciones sin fines de lucro, como clubes o asociaciones, y no cotizan en bolsa. Esto no significa que no puedan constituirse para perseguir fines de lucro, pero no es lo habitual. Al igual que las *public company limited by shares* y *private company limited by shares*, las *companies limited by guaratee* deben inscribirse en la autoridad pertinente (*Registrar of Companies)* y permiten tener socios con diferentes derechos. A diferencia de las sociedades por acciones, a los socios de las *companies limited by guarantee* no se los denomina *shareholders* sino *guarantors* o *members*.

Para finalizar, debemos mencionar las *private unlimited companies*, las cuales se asemejan a las *private company limited by shares*, en tanto son sociedades no cotizadas con estrictos requisitos de constitución, solo que en este caso sus socios tienen responsabilidad ilimitada. Este tipo societario no es muy habitual, puesto que no ofrece ningún tipo de beneficio (ni de responsabilidad ni impositivo). Quienes lo eligen generalmente lo hacen para proteger información, dado que no tienen la obligación de dar a conocer sus cuentas al público. En este caso tampoco los socios son *shareholders* sino *members*.

Problemas de traducción y aspectos pedagógicos

Como pudimos observar tras el breve recorrido por los diferentes tipos societarios utilizados en Argentina e Inglaterra, la primera cuestión que se suscita es de ámbito general. En Argentina existe un único cuerpo legal que recoge todas las formas societarias, el cual está regulado por el denominado Derecho Societario. En Inglaterra y Gales, por su parte, existe una rama del Derecho denominada *Commercial Law*, pero ella no incluye lo que en Argentina denominaríamos Derecho Societario ni concursos y quiebras. Entonces, partimos desde la dificultad de nombrar la rama misma del Derecho que nos convoca. Esto, no obstante, podría resolverse siguiendo las denominaciones utilizadas por los manuales de Derecho ingleses y estadounidenses, en donde se recoge la mayoría de los temas tratados por el Derecho Societario, que generalmente se titulan *Business Law Texbooks* o *Business Organisations Law Texbooks.*

Un primer aspecto terminológico que se presenta, derivado de la denominación "sociedad", es el uso de los adjetivos "social" y "societario" para hacer alusión a las distintas formas. Dado que en Argentina todos los tipos se denominan "sociedades" y aparecen post modificados según sus características, contamos con una única Ley General de Sociedades y los integrantes de todos los tipos societarios se denominan socios. Esto marca una gran diferencia con lo que sucede en Inglaterra y Gales, puesto que para dicha jurisdicción existen dos denominaciones, como vimos: *partnerships* y *companies*, lo que además incide en cómo se nombra a sus miembros y cómo se califican otros sustantivos (por ejemplo, *partnership's address*, *company's address* o *corporate address*).

La traducción inversa de documentos societarios argentinos, así, suscita dificultades terminológicas varias para quienes no estén familiarizados con los tipos societarios y las variantes terminológicas que ellos implican. Este problema, sin embargo, no es privativo de la traducción inversa. Es interesante notar que en las traducciones de los estudiantes suelen detectarse inconvenientes con la traducción del adjetivo *corporate* en frases tales como "*the corporate purpose is...*". El traductor que no está atento a las cuestiones de fondo de los textos o que carece de experiencia en la traducción de textos societarios puede verse tentado a traducir el adjetivo al español como "corporativo", por ejemplo. Si bien el diccionario de la Real Academia Española (s/f) recoge esta voz con la acepción "relativo a una corporación" (defnción 1) y define "corporación" como "una organización compuesta por personas que, como miembros de ella, la gobiernan" (definición 1) o "una empresa, normalmente de grandes dimensiones, en especial si agrupa a otras menores" (definición 2), la legislación argentina no utiliza esta terminología, por lo que consideramos que, en la frase en cuestión, resulta más propio volcar dicho adjetivo como "social" ("el objeto social").

El otro gran problema que siempre aqueja a los traductores, bien sabemos, es el tan ansiado equivalente funcional. Tal como explica Franzoni de Moldavsky (1996: 2), "el concepto de equivalencia es básico para comprender qué implica traducir y es, además, en la práctica profesional, uno de los aspectos que más problemas y divergencias plantea". Chiesa (2016), por su parte, se ha expresado al respecto y ha resaltado que los traductores jurídicos experimentan una especie de obsesión por encontrar equivalencias léxicas, sin importar el género al que pertenezca el texto de trabajo. Así, sostiene este autor, se enseña en la universidad que existe una necesidad imperiosa de hallar equivalentes entre unidades terminológicas que designen conceptos idénticos o semejantes para poder reexpresar las ideas en la lengua meta. En este sentido, tomaremos la propuesta de Mayoral Asensio (2002: 12) para definir el equivalente funcional como "aquel concepto o institución jurídica que cumple el mismo papel en la cultura del texto traducido".

En la traducción de documentos societarios, el primer equivalente que intentamos encontrar es el del tipo societario en cuestión. Para ello es menester primero establecer los rasgos esenciales y los rasgos accesorios de cada una de las figuras, puesto que, según explica Chiesa (2016: 1), solo se alcanza la equivalencia cultural o funcional "cuando la comparación entre esos conceptos atravesados por notas culturales no siempre convergentes [es] satisfactoria desde el punto de vista cualitativo". Esto es, cuando los conceptos en ambas lenguas y sistemas compartes, al menos, la mayoría de los rasgos esenciales y, por qué no, algunos de sus rasgos accesorios.

Como ya dijimos, las diferencias entre las normas de los distintos países derivan de las distintas necesidades y formas de resolverlas de cada sociedad. Esto hace que cada sistema adopte figuras jurídicas únicas y específicas a sus necesidades y patrones culturales. Por consiguiente, sabemos también que es posible que no haya convergencias entre los rasgos esenciales de institutos provenientes de distintos países.

Para el caso de los tipos societarios, creemos que es importante primero determinar cuáles son los rasgos a evaluar. De esta manera, consideramos que será más sencillo encontrar –si existiese– un equivalente funcional.

Este tipo de análisis aplicado a las figuras jurídicas presentes en los textos jurídico-económicos tiene dos claras ventajas para el traductor en formación. En primer lugar, conduce a una comprensión más acabada del instituto por traducir, dado que el desmenuzamiento de los rasgos facilita la visualización y el contraste. Y, por otra parte, a partir de este tipo de análisis, se pueden poner de relieve cuestiones terminológicas contrastivas. A continuación, hemos organizado los rasgos en un cuadro (ver Cuadro 1), a partir del cual podrán establecerse las comparaciones entre distintos tipos societarios. El cuadro toma lo que consideramos son los aspectos prominentes de las sociedades en general y los organiza en dos categorías: rasgos esenciales y rasgos secundarios. La coincidencia en la mayoría de los rasgos principales permitiría establecer una correspondencia entre figuras, la cual puede verse reforzada por la presencia de rasgos secundarios similares. Estos últimos, sin embargo, no serán determinantes a la hora de decidir si dos tipos societarios son o no equivalentes.

Cuadro 1. Modelo para análisis de tipos societarios. Elaboración propia.

Categorías de análisis	**Tipo de sociedad argentina:**	**Tipo de sociedad inglesa:**
Rasgos esenciales		
Tipo de persona		
Forma de constitución		
Responsabilidad de los socios		
Tipos de socios		
Tipos de aportes/capital social		
Rasgos accesorios		
Forma de gobierno/ administración		
Cantidad de socios		
Situación impositiva		
Objeto		

Tomaremos a continuación dos tipos societarios de cada una de las jurisdicciones para evaluar su correspondencia. En primer lugar, analizaremos la posible equivalencia existente entre la sociedad colectiva argentina y la *standard partnership* inglesa.

Cuadro 2. Comparación de la sociedad colectiva argentina y la *standard partnership* de Inglaterra. Elaboración propia.

Categorías de análisis	**Tipo de sociedad argentina: sociedad colectiva**	**Tipo de sociedad inglesa: *standard partnership***
Rasgos esenciales		
Tipo de persona	Persona jurídica	Sin personería
Forma de constitución	Por instrumento público o privado inscripto en el Registro Público	Por instrumento privado o de hecho, sin necesidad de inscripción
Responsabilidad de los socios	Ilimitada y solidaria	Ilimitada y solidaria
Tipos de socios	Un solo tipo de socios	Un solo tipo de socios
Tipos de aportes/capital social	Sociedad de personas – obligaciones de hacer o de dar – partes de interés	Sin obligación legal de hacer aportes al capital – *partnership interest*
Rasgos accesorios		
Forma de gobierno/ administración	Uno o más socios o terceros especificados en el contrato	Todos los socios o quien ellos designen en el el contrato
Cantidad de socios	Dos o más, sin limitación	Dos o más, sin limitación
Situación impositiva	Sujetos al pago de IVA e IIBB, pero no al Impuesto a las Ganancias (pasa directamente a los socios)	No sujeta a impuestos – pasan directamente a los socios.
Objeto	Comercial – fines de lucro	Comercial – fines de lucro

En el cuadro que sigue analizaremos ahora las características básicas de la sociedad anónima argentina, en comparación con los rasgos más prominentes de las las *companies limited by shares* recogidas por la legislación inglesa.

Cuadro 3. Comparación de la sociedad anónima argentina y la *company limited by shares* inglesa. Elaboración propia.

Categorías de análisis	**Tipo de sociedad argentina: sociedad anónima (cotizada/no cotizada)**	**Tipo de sociedad inglesa: public/private company limited by shares**
Rasgos esenciales		
Tipo de persona	Personería jurídica	Personería jurídica
Forma de constitución	Por instrumento público inscripto en el Registro Público (Acta constitutiva y Estatuto)	Por instrumento público inscripto en The Companies House (*Memorandum of association* y *Articles of association*)
Responsabilidad de los socios	limitada	limitada
Tipos de socios	accionistas	Accionistas (*shareholders*)
Tipos de aportes/capital social	acciones	Acciones (*shares*)
Rasgos accesorios		
Forma de gobierno/ administración	Directorio – Asamblea – órgano de fiscalización solo de corresponder	Directorio (*Board of Directors*) – Asamblea (*Meeting of shareholders*) – órgano de fiscalización para sociedades cotizadas (*audit committee*)
Cantidad de socios	Dos o más (nueva posibilidad: SA unipersonal)	Uno o más, sin limitación
Situación impositiva	Sujeta al pago de Impuesto a las Ganancias, IIBB e IVA.	Sujeta al pago de impuesto a las sociedades (*corporation tax*) – socios además sujetos al pago de impuestos individualmente
Objeto	Comercial – fines de lucro	Comercial – con o sin fines de lucro

Como se ha podido observar en ambos cuadros de análisis, los tipos societarios de los dos países comparten suficientes rasgos esenciales (aunque no todos y tampoco todos los accesorios) como para considerarlos equivalentes. Esto, en nuestra opinión, permitiría utilizar las sociedades como equivalentes funcionales. Por el contrario, veremos que no sucede lo mismo con las sociedades que se analizan a continuación:

Cuadro 4. Comparación de la sociedad en comandita por acciones argentina y la *limited partnership* y *company limited by shares* inglesas. Elaboración propia.

Categorías de análisis	**Tipo de sociedad argentina: sociedad en comandita por acciones**	**Tipo de sociedad inglesa: limited partnership**	**Tipo de sociedad inglesa: public/ private company limited by shares**
Rasgos esenciales			
Tipo de persona	Personería jurídica	Sin personería jurídica	Personería jurídica
Forma de constitución	Por instrumento público inscripto en el Registro Público	Por instrumento privado inscripto en The Companies House	Por instrumento público inscripto en The Companies House (*Memorandum of association* y *Articles of association*)
Responsabilidad de los socios	Según tipo de socio: limitada e ilimitada y solidaria	Según tipo de socio: limitada e ilimitada y solidaria	limitada
Tipos de socios	Socio comanditario y socio comanditado	Socio comanditario (*limited partner*) y socio comanditado (*general partner*)	Accionistas (*shareholders*)
Tipos de aportes/ capital social	Acciones	Sin obligación legal de hacer aportes al capital – *partnership interest*	Acciones (*shares*)

Cuadro 4. Continúa

Categorías de análisis	**Tipo de sociedad argentina: sociedad en comandita por acciones**	**Tipo de sociedad inglesa: limited partnership**	**Tipo de sociedad inglesa: public/ private company limited by shares**
Rasgos accesorios			
Forma de gobierno/ administración	Administración por el/los socios comanditarios o tercero (posibilidad de administración unipersonal)	Administración por el/los socios comanditarios o tercero	Directorio (*Board of Directors*) – Asamblea(*Meeting ofshareholders*)– órgano de fiscalización para sociedades cotizadas (*audit committee*)
Cantidad de socios	Mínimo dos (uno de cada tipo)	Mínimo dos (uno de cada tipo)	Uno o más, sin limitación
Situación impositiva	Sujeta al pago de Impuesto a las Ganancias, IIBB e IVA.	No sujeta a pago de impuestos – cada socio paga individualmente	Sujeta al pago de impuesto a las sociedades (*corporation tax*) – socios además sujetos al pago de impuestos individualmente
Objeto	Comercial – fines de lucro	Comercial – fines de lucro	Comercial – con o sin fines de lucro

Cuando se intenta identificar el equivalente funcional de la sociedad en comandita por acciones argentina, para su traducción al inglés de Inglaterra, nos encontramos con que el ordenamiento jurídico del país sajón no cuenta con ninguna estructura societaria que comparte todos –ni la mayoría– de los rasos esenciales. En realidad, la sociedad argentina en cuestión comparte algunos rasgos esenciales con la *limited partnership* inglesa y otros con las *companies limited by shares*. La correcta detección de esta información debería permitirle al traductor crear una etiqueta que dé cuenta de las características fundamentales de las sociedades, con el fin de evitar posibles errores de interpretación en el texto meta.

Centrándonos ahora en el plano pedagógico, quisiéramos resaltar que, en nuestra opinión, este tipo de análisis no se limita a las formas societarias y, sin lugar a dudas, podría replicarse con otras categorías problemáticas. Consideramos que este modelo de análisis redunda en un gran beneficio para los traductores en formación, al brindar herramientas replicables ante situaciones nuevas y conceptos desconocidos.

Como hemos planteado en otras oportunidades (Amorebieta y Vera, Munch y Remiro 2019a, 2019b, 2020, 2022; Espósito y Amorebieta y Vera, 2020; Remiro y Amorebieta y Vera, 2022; Munch y Remiro, 2022; y Amorebieta y Vera, Espósito, Munch y Remiro, 2023), los estudiantes de traducción se ven favorecidos por la adopción de un enfoque progresivo en el acercamiento a la traducción especializada, en tanto esta forma de abordaje fomenta la adquisición de las habilidades y competencias necesarias para todo traductor. Esta clase de análisis, en la cual se desmenuzan las figuras para comprenderlas y compararlas, constituye un recurso sumamente útil a la hora enseñar una manera de arribar al tan deseado equivalente y permite, además, visualizar las diferencias culturales para que, cuando no exista equivalente, puedan evaluarse otras técnicas o estrategias de traducción aplicables.

Tal como sostiene Feldman (2010: 16), "enseñar es permitir que dos personas sepan lo que al principio sabía una sola". El objetivo de la educación superior es sortear esa desigualdad inicial y formar profesionales que, finalizado el ciclo, se convertirán en colegas. Lejos estamos hoy de la creencia que sostenía que se aprende a traducir únicamente traduciendo. Para formar traductores competentes es necesario diseñar tareas y actividades que posibiliten, por un lado, la reflexión acerca de lo que implica traducir y, por otro, la adquisición progresiva de los conocimientos que exige el correcto desempeño de la tarea.

En este caso en particular, nos hemos centrado en los conocimientos extralingüísticos necesarios para traducir textos concernientes a las sociedades comerciales de Argentina e Inglaterra. Si bien podría suponerse que con la simple lectura de la legislación aplicable o con la explicación docente de las formas societarias puede bastar para que los estudiantes adquieran las nociones básicas para comprender los textos y encontrar los equivalentes necesarios, la experiencia docente nos indica que la creación de tareas posibilitadoras que pongan en foco en la construcción de conocimientos autónomo por parte del estudiantado redunda en mayores beneficios educativos. A partir del trabajo de lectura, investigación, análisis y comparación, los estudiantes llegan a una mayor comprensión temática, por supuesto; pero, además, adquieren las herramientas necesarias para justificar sus decisiones de traducción –otro de los aspectos que consideramos clave en la formación de traductores– y descartar opciones de traducción poco adecuadas.

El tipo de trabajo que planteamos puede realizarse en clase o puede solicitarse con anterioridad para ser revisado en clase, según las horas de contacto semanal que tenga la materia y la necesidad de acompañamiento que detecte el docente en el grupo de estudiantes. Resulta conveniente aclarar, también, que es posible que sea necesario guiar a los estudiantes en la realización del cuadro la primera vez que se aborda este tipo de actividad, de manera de mostrar qué tanto detalle es relevante registrar. Esto permitirá que los estudiantes ganen independencia y puedan realizar este mismo tipo de tareas de forma autónoma e, incluso, que puedan replicarlas cuando se trabaje con otros temas o documentos.

La confección de cuadros de la naturaleza planteada aquí, además, exige a los estudiantes la lectura de bibliografía especializada en sus lenguas de trabajo, lo que proporciona una importante exposición al lenguaje de especialidad que deberán utilizar en sus traducciones. La lectura de material bibliográfico permitirá que los estudiantes se familiaricen con la fraseología y la terminología propia del campo, lo que a su vez posibilitará –sin lugar a dudas– el desarrollo de distintos tipos de actividades lingüísticas relacionadas y favorecedoras para la traducción.

Las tareas de análisis previas a la traducción brindan, así, un andamiaje clave para el desarrollo de la competencia traductora. Como ya dijimos, el conocimiento del campo es un factor fundamental en toda rama de traducción especializada y la traducción económica no es la excepción. El diseño, entonces, de material que propenda a la adquisición de este tipo de conocimiento no podrá sino redundar en beneficios, los que sin duda se traducirán en un mejor rendimiento académico y profesional.

Reflexiones finales

Esta contribución ha pretendido analizar las posibles equivalencias (o inequivalencias) entre las figuras societarias de Argentina e Inglaterra, los problemas terminológicos que se suscitan y las implicancias que todo ello tiene en la enseñanza de la traducción especializada en las clases de Traducción Jurídica y Económica en inglés 2 en la Universidad Nacional de La Plata, Argentina. Para ello se describieron y analizaron los diferentes tipos societarios existentes en los países seleccionados, echando mano de las herramientas provistas por el derecho comparado; se establecieron posibles equivalencias, a partir de un análisis de los rasgos esenciales y accesorios de cada una; y se comparó la terminología propia del campo en ambas lenguas.

En el transcurso de estas comparaciones, hemos detectado, como es de esperar, problemas tanto a nivel semántico como a nivel léxico. Creemos que el tipo de análisis propuesto, al ser correctamente explotado en las clases de traducción, propende a hallar vías para la solución las dificultades evidenciadas por los estudiantes. El objetivo último es siempre contribuir a la formación de profesionales capaces, que desarrollen autonomía y adquieran hábitos replicables ante situaciones inesperadas.

Es claro que la no identificación o incluso la identificación incorrecta de los rasgos esenciales de los institutos jurídicos presentes en los documentos por traducir deriva indefectiblemente en problemas de traducción. Sin embargo, estos problemas no sólo tienen consecuencias textuales, al acarrear errores de sentido, por ejemplo, sino también pueden traer consecuencias jurídicas y económico-financieras para el cliente o para el usuario de la traducción.

Los documentos de índole jurídico-económica, sabemos, son eminentemente operativos. Se redactan para cumplir con una función en una sociedad dada. La traducción incorrecta de las figuras jurídicas en ellos presentes, entonces, puede derivar en un cambio de función en el texto meta, lo que a su vez puede afectar la operatividad de la traducción y entorpecer las acciones por las que se ha encomendado la traducción. Creemos, entonces, que el desarrollo de técnicas que garanticen un acercamiento acabado al texto de origen y la adquisición de herramientas de comparación permitirán que tanto los traductores en formación como los profesionales en ejercicio puedan garantizar traducciones jurídico-económicas de calidad y adecuadas a los fines para los que se los contacta.

Referencias bibliográficas

Alcalde Peñalver, E. (2016). La doble especialización en traducción jurídica y financiera: vínculos y necesidades formativas en España. *MonTI. Monografías de Traducción e Interpretación,* 8: 279–300.

Amorebieta y Vera, J., Munch, M. & Remiro, G. (2019a). La utilidad del enfoque por tareas y de la noción de género discursivo en la didáctica de la traducción jurídica. *Belas Infeis*, 8(2): 13–30.

Amorebieta y Vera, J., Munch, M. & Remiro, G. (2019b). Derecho comparado y traducción: una propuesta de aplicación áulica. In AA.VV. *Ponencias presentadas en el II Congreso de Traductorado, celebrado los días 22, 23 y 24 de abril de 2019 en CABA. UBA, Argentina,* 3–18. Descargable de: http://www.derecho.uba.ar/publicaciones/libros/ind-ponencias-presentadas-caba.php

Amorebieta y Vera, J., Munch, M. & Remiro, G. (2020). Derecho comparado como herramienta para la comprensión de textos en la clase de traducción jurídica. In C. Giordano & G. Morandi (Eds.), *Memorias de las 3° Jornadas sobre las prácticas docentes en la Universidad Pública. El proyecto político académico de la Educación Superior en el contexto nacional y regional.*

Amorebieta y Vera, J., Munch, M. & Remiro, G. (2022). La utilidad de las tareas de traducción en la clase de Traducción Jurídica: un estudio de caso. In *V Jornadas Internacionales de Traductología: "Perspectivas en Diálogo"*, organizada por el Área de Traductología (ATRA) del centro de Investigaciones de la Facultad de Lenguas, Universidad Nacional de Córdoba, Argentina, 31 de julio, 1 y 2 de agosto de 2019.

Amorebieta y Vera, J., Espósito, J., Munch, M. & Remiro, G. (2023). El equivalente funcional en la traducción jurídica: Reflexiones sobre su uso y conveniencia de utilización. In A. Beatriz Cagnolati & L. Spoturno (Eds.), *Problemas de traducción. Enfoques plurales para su identificación y tratamiento*. Editorial de la Universidad Nacional de La Plata (EDULP). Capítulo de libro aceptado para su publicación.

Chiesa, R. (2016). Visibilidad del traductor jurídico: el caso de la equivalencia aparente. Ponencia presentada en el VI Congreso Latinoamericano de Traducción e Interpretación. *El traductor después del mañana*, organizado por el Colegio de Traductores Públicos de la Ciudad de Buenos Aires, del 21 al 24 de abril de 2016.

Espósito, J. & Amorebieta y Vera, J. (2020). El derecho comparado como método en la enseñanza- aprendizaje de la traducción jurídica en Argentina. *Veritas & Research*, 2(1): 27–36.

Franzoni de Moldavsky, A. (1996). La equivalencia funcional en traducción jurídica. *Voces 20, Revista Oficial del Colegio de Traductores Públicos de la Ciudad de Buenos Aires,* 2–13.

Feldman, D. (2010). *Didáctica General.* Ministerio de Educación de la Nación.

Gallego Hernández, D., Koby, G. & Román Martínez, V. (2016). Economic, financial, and commercial translation: An approach to theoretical aspects. A survey- based study. *MonTI. Monografías de Traducción e Interpretación,* 8: 35–59.

García Izquierdo, I. (2005). *El género textual y la traducción: reflexiones teóricas y aplicaciones pedagógicas.* Bern: Peter Lang.

Mayoral Asensio, R. (2002). ¿Cómo se hace la traducción jurídica? *Puentes* 2: 9–14.

Mayoral Asensio, R. (2007). La traducción comercial. In P. Fuertes-Olivera (Ed.), *Problemas lingüísticos en la traducción especializada* (pp. 33–47). Universidad de Valladolid.

Nissen, R. (2019). *Curso de derecho societario* (3ra. Edición). Hammurabi.

Prieto Ramos, F. (2021). Translating legal terminology and phraseology: Between inter- systemic incongruity and multilingual harmonization. *Perspectives*, 29(2): 175–183.

Real Academia Española. (s.f.). Cultura. *Diccionario de la lengua española.*

Remiro, G. & Amorebieta y Vera, J. (2022). La Creación de Material Bibliográfico para la Enseñanza de la traducción jurídica en Argentina: del Desafío a la Realidad. *Trayectorias Universitarias*, 8(14).

Socorro Trujillo, K. (2016). La enseñanza de la traducción comercial (inglés-español): una propuesta formativa. *MonTI,* 8: 257–268.

Vittolo, D. (2016). *Manual de Derecho Comercial.* Editorial Estudio.

François Maniez

4 Traduction automatique des trigrammes nominaux (anglais/français/anglais) dans la langue spécialisée de l'économie

Translation of English noun phrases featuring head modification shows a high degree of variation when translating into Romance languages, with modifiers' "unpacking" (Gledhill & Pecman, 2015) as noun complements introduced by various prepositions. In English for Specific Purposes, double nominal premodification produces trigrams whose translation into Romance languages mostly uses the prepositions *de* or *di*. In the process of back-translation from Romance languages into English, machine translation of such noun phrases may be partially or totally literal, and therefore does not systematically restore head modification (*highest income category cut-off →seuil de la catégorie de revenu la plus élevée →threshold for the highest income category*). After selecting trinominal economic terms from the Social Sciences part of the Corpus of Contemporary American English (Davies, 2009), we study differences in the results obtained by two machine translation programs (Google Translate and DeepL). In particular, a study of back-translation into English shows that a significantly higher rate of nominal trigrams is restored in back-translation by DeepL, and that the degree of trigram restoration depends on their frequency of use in the source language, as well as on the complexity of the noun phrases in which they are embedded.

Introduction

Les bigrammes dans lesquels un nom (N1) prémodifie un autre nom (N2) en anglais donnent fréquemment lieu à une traduction contenant un groupe prépositionnel dans les langues romanes, où l'on observe généralement dans les équivalents de traduction (désormais ET) utilisés le développement des éléments prémodificateurs sous la forme d'un complément de nom. La préposition *de* est le plus souvent employée en français (*blood donor/donneur de sang*), la même structure étant employée en espagnol (*donador de sangre*) et en italien (*donatore di sangue*).

Mais comme l'ont souligné Gledhill et Pecman (2018), les deux structures en question (prémodification/ complémentation) peuvent désigner le même référent en anglais, où l'on observe des alternances telles que *aspirin synthesis /synthesis of aspirin* pour lesquelles Gledhill & Pecman emploient respectivement les adjectifs *packed* et *unpacked* (on pourrait également citer comme exemple le choix entre les formes *cell proliferation* et *proliferation of cells*). L'un des problèmes de la traduction automatique (désormais TA) du français vers l'anglais est d'ailleurs l'absence fréquente de *repacking* lors du passage des langues romanes à l'anglais, qui se manifeste par l'utilisation par défaut de la complémentation par imitation de la structure de la langue source (N de N).

L'opacité de la relation entre les deux noms anglais pose également le problème du choix de la préposition lors de la traduction vers le français, cas dans lequel la préposition *de* est souvent employée par défaut en TA. Or, comme le montrent les quelques exemples de variation de la préposition dans la traduction française de bigrammes lexicalisés ci-dessous, de nombreuses autres possibilités existent :

- pocket money/argent **de** poche
- water pistol/pistolet **à** eau
- bank account/compte **en** banque
- wheel drive/entraînement **par** roue
- mound culture/culture **sur** buttes
- greenhouse cultivation/culture **sous/en** serre

L'explicitation de la relation entre les deux noms consécutifs de la structure anglaise N1 N2 par l'emploi de la préposition adéquate constitue pour le traducteur un choix délicat. Ainsi, dans la traduction française du groupe nominal *A High Court legal challenge against Brexit* (Tableau 1), l'utilisation de la préposition *de* ou *par* dans les traductions successives de Google Translate (désormais GT) est une erreur, et c'est la préposition *devant*, présente dans la traduction proposée par DeepL (désormais DL) qui exprime le mieux la relation entre l'entité nommée *High Court* et le groupe nominal qu'elle modifie, *legal challenge*.

Tableau 1. Traductions du groupe nominal *A High Court legal challenge against Brexit* par les programmes de TA Google Translate (GT) et DeepL (DL)

Programme de TA	**Traduction**
GT 2019	Une contestation judiciaire **de** la Haute Cour contre le Brexit
GT 2021	Une contestation judiciaire **par** la Haute Cour contre le Brexit
DL 2019	Un recours en justice **devant** la Haute Cour contre Brexit

On observe également une variation des traductions pour ce qui est du nombre (comme dans le cas de *horse race* et *horse manure* respectivement traduits par *course de* ***chevaux*** et *crottin de* ***cheval***) ainsi que pour la détermination, avec 3 ET fréquemment utilisés pour *tumor growth* (*croissance [d'une tumeur/de la tumeur/des tumeurs]*) en cas de complémentation, et une quatrième solution consistant en l'utilisation d'un adjectif relationnel (*croissance tumorale*), fréquente en langue spécialisée.

Il n'est pas rare que les groupes nominaux de la langue scientifique comportent un grand nombre d'éléments prémodificateurs. En anglais, le fait que ces éléments prémodificateurs ne subissent pas de flexion augmente leur représentation statistique dans les corpus par rapport à leurs ET dans les langues romanes, qui sont davantage susceptibles de se présenter sous des formes diverses, notamment pour ce qui concerne la détermination. A titre d'exemple, le quadrigramme *tumor growth inhibition effect* compte plus de 800 occurrences sur le moteur de recherche Google Scholar (désormais GS), alors que l'ET renvoyé par DL et GT (*effet inhibiteur de la croissance tumorale*) n'en compte que trois (outre la variation des traductions françaises, cet écart considérable s'explique bien sûr également par le fait que l'anglais soit devenu la *lingua franca* de la recherche scientifique).

Comme le montrent les données résumées dans le Tableau 2, la forme la plus fréquemment employée en français (*effet d'inhibition de la croissance tumorale*) est celle dans laquelle le nom *inhibition* est traduit non pas littéralement mais par un adjectif relationnel. Mais le fait que cette forme semble avoir moins de chances d'être utilisée par les logiciels de TA pourrait être dû à la prépondérance de la traduction française *inhibition de la croissance tumorale* pour le trigramme initial de ce terme, *tumor growth inhibition*, en comparaison avec l'utilisation relativement plus rare de l'adjectif relationnel *inhibiteur* dans *inhibiteur de la croissance tumorale.*

Tableau 2. Fréquence d'utilisation des traductions du groupe nominal *tumor growth inhibition (effect)* sur le moteur de recherche Google Scholar (GS)

Groupe nominal anglais	Traduction	Fréquence (GS)
tumor growth inhibition	inhibition de la croissance tumorale	49
tumor growth inhibition	inhibiteur de la croissance tumorale	73
tumor growth inhibition effect	effet d'inhibition de la croissance tumorale	3
tumor growth inhibition effect	effet inhibiteur de la croissance tumorale	10

L'emploi d'un adjectif relationnel dans la traduction de ce type de terme complexe n'est pas exclusivement l'apanage du français. L'utilisation d'un adjectif pour traduire le nom *inhibition* dans le terme *tumor growth inhibition effect* est également majoritaire en espagnol sur GS, où les ET *efecto inhibidor del crecimiento tumoral* et *efecto inhibitorio del crecimiento tumoral* sont 8 fois plus fréquemment employés que le groupe nominal utilisant la traduction de *inhibition* par un nom, *efecto de inhibición del crecimiento tumoral.* En allemand, l'utilisation du groupe nominal comprenant une forme adjectivale issue du participe présent du verbe *hemmen* (*Tumorwachstum hemmende Wirkung,* forme proposée par DL), est également deux fois plus fréquente que celle du groupe nominal *Hemmwirkung auf das Tumorwachstum* (également proposé par DL), dans lequel on observe un regroupement en deux bigrammes correspondant respectivement à *inhibition effect* et à *tumor growth.* Le fait que l'équivalent choisi par GT (*Hemmwirkung des Tumorwachstums*) soit inusité sur GS pourrait être dû au choix d'une complémentation en *des* par défaut, équivalente à celle du français quand il utilise la préposition *de.*

Comme dans les autres langues de spécialité, les cas de double prémodification nominale dans la langue de l'économie produisent en anglais des trigrammes dont la traduction en langues romanes utilise majoritairement une complémentation par la préposition *de/di* (*income redistribution policies/politiques de redistribution des revenus/políticas de redistribución de la renta/politiche di redistribuzione del reddito*). Lors du passage des langues romanes vers l'anglais, la traduction automatique des groupes nominaux contenant de tels compléments de nom peut être partiellement ou totalement littérale, et ne reproduit donc pas systématiquement la structure de la prémodification nominale, comme peuvent le prouver des tests de rétrotraduction (*highest income category cut-off →seuil de la catégorie de revenu la plus élevée →threshold for the highest income category*).

Dans la prose scientifique, bon nombre de séquences binominales ou trinominales sont des termes dont la traduction varie peu, voire pas du tout. Mais quand ces séquences ne sont pas lexicalisées, la variation de l'usage, logiquement reflétée par les mémoires de traduction, l'est également dans les résultats de la TA. Devant la grande diversité des résultats renvoyés par celle-ci, nous tenterons dans ce qui suit de répondre aux deux questions suivantes à propos des résultats de la TA dans le domaine de l'économie :

1. À partir de quel degré de complexité des groupes nominaux la restitution des GN sans préposition (*repacking*) est-elle moins fréquente ?
2. L'un des deux programmes offre-t-il une meilleure restitution des GN trinominaux (NNN) ?

Corpus et méthode

Pour la préselection des termes économiques trinominaux, nous avons utilisé la partie consacrée aux articles de recherche en sciences sociales (*Social Sciences*) du sous-corpus *Academic* (un peu plus de 120 millions de mots) du Corpus de l'américain contemporain (COCA, Davies, 2009), qui compte un peu plus d'un milliard de mots.

Nous avons dans un premier temps extrait les termes économiques binominaux débutant par un certain nombre de mots clés du vocabulaire économique tels que *consumer*, *income*, *inflation* ou *tax*. Nous avons ensuite effectué une recherche portant sur les trigrammes débutant par ces bigrammes (*consumer goods industries*, *income replacement insurance, inflation target range, tax cut package*). Nous avons enfin extrait les phrases contenant ces trigrammes afin d'étudier leur traitement par les deux programmes de TA cités plus haut (GT et DL). Pour des raisons de rapidité de traitement, et dans la mesure où les modèles de la TA traitent généralement les phrases de manière isolée (Tiedemann et Scherrer, 2017), les phrases que nous avions extraites du corpus ont été isolées de leur contexte. Il faut cependant signaler que la TA neuronale semble depuis quelques années commencer à tenir compte du contexte amont au-delà du niveau de la phrase (Maniez, 2017; Voita et al., 2019), si bien que le résultat obtenu aurait pu être différent si une portion du contexte amont avait été fournie lors de l'interrogation de ces logiciels de traduction en ligne.

Résultats obtenus pour la traduction des trigrammes

Le Tableau 2 donne un exemple des résultats obtenus lors de l'extraction des trigrammes débutant par le bigramme *income tax*.

Tableau 3. Trigrammes débutant par le bigramme *income tax* dans la partie *Social Sciences* du Corpus de l'américain contemporain

Trigramme	Fréquence
income tax credit	480
income tax rates	422
income tax rate	408
income tax return	218
income tax system	91
income tax purposes	71
[...]	
income tax work	2
income tax theories	2

Pour notre étude, nous avons choisi de privilégier les trigrammes de faible fréquence. En effet, dans la mesure où ceux dont la fréquence est la plus élevée sont très souvent des termes de la langue spécialisée de l'économie ou de la finance, leur traduction n'est guère susceptible de variation. A titre d'exemple, à l'exception du terme *income tax credit*, tous les trigrammes de haute fréquence du Tableau 3 sont des termes recensés sur la base de données terminologique Termium Plus (*income tax rate* : taux d'imposition du revenu, *income tax return* : déclaration de revenus, *income tax system* : régime d'impôt sur le revenu, *for income tax purposes* : aux fins du calcul de l'impôt).

A l'inverse, des trigrammes de faible fréquence d'utilisation tels que *income tax theories* pourront être traduits différemment par les deux programmes de TA, voire par le même programme s'ils figurent dans deux phrases distinctes. Le Tableau 4 fait ainsi apparaître le traitement très différent d'une phrase contenant ce trigramme par les deux logiciels, et sa conséquence sur la rétrotraduction du groupe nominal vers l'anglais : chez GT, l'introduction de la préposition *de* dans le groupe prépositionnel *de l'impôt sur le revenu* (unpacking) donne lieu à l'adoption de la même structure à la rétrotraduction (*of income tax*). En revanche, la traduction française de DL pour *income tax* utilise le seul adjectif *fiscal*, ce qui donne lieu à la rétrotraduction à l'emploi du nom *tax*, et à la disparition de son prémodificateur *income*.

Tableau 4. Traduction française et rétrotraduction vers l'anglais du trigramme *income tax theories* dans la partie *Social Sciences* du Corpus de l'américain contemporain

Texte source	Traduction GT	Rétrotrad. GT	Traduction DL	Rétrotrad. DL
[...] to submit tax returns based on false **income tax theories.**	[...] à soumettre des déclarations de revenus basées sur de fausses **théories de l'impôt sur le revenu.**	[...] to submit tax returns based on false **theories of income tax.**	[...] à soumettre des déclarations de revenus basées sur de **fausses théories fiscales.**	[...] to file tax returns based on **false tax theories.**

Outre ces différences concernant la construction syntaxique utilisée pour la traduction des groupes trinominaux, on observe également certaines variations lexicales lors du processus de rétrotraduction. Ces variations sont probablement dues au fait que la TA neuronale recourt à des corpus de très grande taille dans la langue cible (ce qui a d'ailleurs grandement contribué à l'amélioration de la fluidité des traductions), si bien que des groupes nominaux d'emploi relativement rares sont susceptibles d'être remplacés par d'autres dont la fréquence d'utilisation est supérieure. Le Tableau 5 fournit un exemple d'une telle variation lexicale pour le terme *income continuation insurance*, auquel se substitue à la rétrotraduction le terme *income maintenance insurance*.

Tableau 5. Traduction française et rétrotraduction vers l'anglais du trigramme *income continuation insurance* dans la partie *Social Sciences* du Corpus de l'américain contemporain

Texte source	Traduction GT	Rétrotrad. GT	Traduction DL	Rétrotrad. DL
But disaster insurance should provide you with a component of **income continuation insurance** [...].	Mais l'assurance en cas de catastrophe devrait vous fournir une composante d'une **assurance de maintien du revenu** [...].	But disaster insurance should provide you with a component of **income maintenance insurance** [...].	Mais l'assurance contre les catastrophes devrait vous fournir un élément d'**assurance de maintien du revenu** [...].	But catastrophic insurance should provide you with an element of **income maintenance insurance** [...].

Si l'on compare les fréquences d'occurrence observées pour les deux trigrammes sur le moteur de recherche Google (consulté le 03/06/2023), le résultat obtenu ne semble pas indiquer une très nette préférence pour l'une ou l'autre forme, la requête "*income continuation insurance*" donnant 40 résultats contre 65 pour "*income maintenance insurance*". En revanche, la consultation des chiffres obtenus pour les bigrammes initiaux de ces deux groupes nominaux révèle une différence beaucoup plus significative quant à leurs fréquences d'emploi : la requête "*income continuation*" donne un peu plus de 63 000 résultats, contre 814 000 pour "*income maintenance*". Dans la mesure où les vecteurs de mots utilisés par la TA reflètent les statistiques concernant l'emploi des cooccurrents immédiats dans la langue cible, il est probable que cette différence significative (ratio voisin de 13) est à l'origine du choix opéré par les deux programmes de TA.

Sur les 150 trigrammes nominaux traduits, la rétrotraduction a donné lieu à la restitution du trigramme du texte source dans 97 cas (65 %) chez GT et dans 129 cas (86 %) chez DL. Cette différence relativement conséquente demanderait à être confirmée à plus grande échelle et dans d'autres langues de spécialité.

Résultats obtenus pour les groupes nominaux de taille supérieure

Ayant observé de manière empirique que le taux de restitution du groupe nominal du texte source à la rétrotraduction semblait diminuer quand la longueur et la complexité du groupe nominal augmentaient, nous étudierons ici quelques exemples de quadrigrammes et de structures syntaxiques complexes.

L'exemple du Tableau 6 fait apparaître un cas de variation lexicale similaire à celui du tableau précédent, la rétrotraduction de *wage deduction payment plan* donnant lieu à sa transformation en *payroll deduction payment plan.*

Tableau 6. Traduction française et rétrotraduction vers l'anglais du quadrigramme *wage deduction payment plan* dans la partie *Social Sciences* du Corpus de l'américain contemporain

Texte source	Traduction GT	Rétrotrad. GT	Traduction DL	Rétrotrad. DL
In Ontario, the only province to enact such legislation, a **wage deduction payment plan** [...].	En Ontario, la seule province à adopter une telle législation, un **plan de paiement des retenues sur les salaires** [...].	In Ontario, the only province to pass such legislation, a **payroll deduction payment plan** [...].	En Ontario, la seule province à avoir adopté une telle législation, un **plan de paiement par retenue sur le salaire** [...].	In Ontario, the only province with such legislation, a **payroll deduction payment plan** [...].

Après comparaison des fréquences d'occurrence observées pour les deux quadrigrammes sur le moteur de recherche Google (consulté le 03/06/2023), le résultat obtenu indique une préférence pour la forme adoptée à la rétrotraduction par les deux programmes (*payroll deduction payment plan*) avec 49 résultats, contre seulement 3 pour le quadrigramme du texte source (*wage deduction payment plan*). Mais là encore, la consultation des chiffres obtenus pour les bigrammes initiaux de ces deux groupes nominaux révèle une différence bien plus significative, la requête "*wage deduction*" donnant 373 000 résultats contre 2 430 000 pour "*payroll deduction*", soit un ratio supérieur à 6. Notons au passage que la variation des traductions françaises (plan de paiement **des retenues sur les salaires/** plan de paiement **par retenue sur le salaire**) n'empêche pas la restitution de quadrigrammes identiques à la rétrotraduction vers l'anglais.

Un autre phénomène fréquemment observé lors de la traduction et de la rétrotraduction des quadrigrammes est l'ellipse de l'un de leurs constituants. Dans l'exemple du Tableau 7, cette ellipse se produit même en deux occasions avec DL : non seulement *employee* remplace *wage earner* qui figurait dans le texte source, mais *bankruptcy filings*, simplement traduit en français par « faillites », donne le seul nom *bankruptcies* à la rétrotraduction.

Tableau 7. Traduction française et rétrotraduction vers l'anglais du quadrigramme *wage earner bankruptcy filings* dans la partie *Social Sciences* du Corpus de l'américain contemporain

Texte source	Traduction GT	Rétrotrad. GT	Traduction DL	Rétrotrad. DL
In 1928, there were three reported **wage earner bankruptcy filings.**	En 1928, trois **dépôts de bilan de salariés** ont été signalés.	In 1928, three **employee bankruptcy filings** were reported.	En 1928, trois **faillites de salariés** ont été signalées.	In 1928, three **employee bankruptcies** were reported.

On observe cependant à la fois une similitude des traductions françaises et une stabilité à la restitution des quadrigrammes du texte source quand leur structure syntaxique consiste en une association de deux bigrammes préconstruits, structure qui pourrait se résumer par le découpage [AB] [CD]. C'est le cas de dans la phrase suivante :

Infrastructure spending and rapid urbanization trends are also important growth drivers for emerging- market consumer spending, which should keep **wage rate growth trends** above those of developed markets for some time.

Notons au passage que le groupe nominal *emerging- market consumer spending* est de structure similaire, mais que l'utilisation du trait d'union rend cette structure encore plus claire à la lecture, tout en posant en revanche des problèmes de détection automatique dans le cadre de l'utilisation des corpus. Le Tableau 8 fait apparaître une parfaite similitude des deux opérations de traduction chez GT et DL.

Tableau 8. Traduction française et rétrotraduction vers l'anglais du quadrigramme *wage rate growth trends* dans la partie *Social Sciences* du Corpus de l'américain contemporain

Texte source	Traduction GT	Rétrotrad. GT	Traduction DL	Rétrotrad. DL
[...] keep **wage rate growth trends** above those of developed markets.	[...] maintenir les **tendances de croissance des taux de salaire** au-dessus de celles des marchés développés.	[...] keep **wage rate growth trends** above those in developed markets.	[...] maintenir les **tendances de croissance des taux de salaire** au-dessus de celles des marchés développés.	[...] keep **wage rate growth trends** above those in developed markets.

Si une telle stabilité s'observe généralement pour les quadrigrammes de découpage [AB] [CD], il n'en va pas de même pour les structures faisant intervenir trois opérations de prémodification successives, ce qui est le cas de *[[wage sector] job] dreams* dans l'énoncé suivant :

As **wage sector job dreams** die, young men in their thousands, many of them school dropouts, are selling small consumer items at the roadside – a veritable growth sector !

L'examen du Tableau 9 révèle que de telles structures sont susceptibles d'une plus grande variation pour les deux opérations successives de traduction, et que l'emploi des groupes prépositionnels à la rétrotraduction y est plus fréquent.

Tableau 9. Traduction française et rétrotraduction vers l'anglais du quadrigramme *wage sector job dreams* dans la partie *Social Sciences* du Corpus de l'américain contemporain

Texte source	Traduction GT	Rétrotrad. GT	Traduction DL	Rétrotrad. DL
As wage sector job dreams die [...]	Alors que les rêves d'emploi dans le secteur salarié meurent, [...]	As "dreams of employment in the salaried sector" die, [...]	Alors que les **rêves d'emplois salariés** s'éteignent, [...]	As dreams of wage employment fade, [...]

Comme nous l'avons dit plus haut, les statistiques de cooccurrence des bigrammes et des trigrammes inclus dans les groupes nominaux complexes du texte source jouent certainement un rôle important pour leur restitution lors de la rétrotraduction. Les résultats obtenus sur le moteur de recherche Google (consulté le 03/06/2023) pour les constituants des deux quadrigrammes *wage rate growth trends* et *wage sector job dreams* et pour les divers groupes nominaux qui les constituent sont de ce point de vue révélateurs, les résultats de la TA s'appuyant fondamentalement sur les statistiques concernant l'emploi de cooccurrents immédiats dans la langue cible.

Tableau 10. Fréquence observée sur le moteur de recherche Google des bigrammes et des trigrammes inclus dans les groupes nominaux *wage rate growth trends* et *wage sector job dreams*

Séquence	Constituants	Google	Constituants	Google
ABCD	"wage rate growth trends"	1	"wage sector job dreams"	1
ABC	"wage rate growth"	16 200	"wage sector job"	55
BCD	"rate growth trends"	74	"sector job dreams"	1
AB	"wage rate"	5 310 000	"wage sector"	167 000
CD	"growth trends"	6 630 000	"job dreams"	274 000

L'examen du tableau révèle tout d'abord que les deux quadrigrammes sont des hapax sur Google, ce qui signifie que les uniques occurrences qui y ont été relevées sont celles des articles inclus dans le corpus de l'américain contemporain. Mais on observe également que les séquences correspondant aux deux premiers mots (AB) et aux deux derniers mots (CD) du quadrigramme sont respectivement 32 et 24 fois plus fréquemment utilisées sur la Toile pour *wage rate growth trends* que pour *wage sector job dreams*. Quant au trigramme initial (ABC), *wage rate growth* est près de 300 fois plus fréquemment utilisé que *wage sector job*. Ces statistiques pourraient expliquer le fait que *wage rate growth trends* ait été restitué à la rétrotraduction par les deux programmes de TA, contrairement à *wage sector job dreams*.

Quand les quadrigrammes nominaux sont inclus dans des GN de taille supérieure, comme c'est le cas dans l'exemple du Tableau 11 (*that poor minimum wage call center fellow*), la restitution de la totalité des opérations de prémodification (*repacking*) n'est pas systématique. Voici l'énoncé original :

Of course the politicians are far more complicit and well paid than that poor **minimum wage call center fellow** on the receiving end of your invective, but you lash out at the ones you can see or reach....

Le quadrigramme initial de cet énoncé peut être considéré comme étant d'une structure syntaxique similaire à celles des deux GN dont la traduction a été commentée dans le Tableau 9 (*[minimum wage] [call center] fellow*). La préservation de ce quadrigramme à la rétrotraduction reflète là encore les résultats obtenus sur Google pour ses deux composants (plusieurs dizaines de millions d'occurrences pour *minimum wage* et *call center*). En revanche, le groupe prépositionnel introduit par *du* dans les deux traductions françaises est conservé à la rétrotraduction (GN introduit par *at*), ce qui a pour conséquence de désambiguïser aussi bien l'énoncé initial que sa traduction française, dans lesquels *minimum wage* pouvait prémodifier soit *call center* soit *fellow*. Quelle que soit la structure syntaxique gouvernant le sens de l'énoncé original, il est fort probable que la traduction française serait perçue par des locuteurs natifs comme faisant intervenir un rattachement du groupe prépositionnel *au salaire minimum* à *gars* plutôt qu'à *centre d'appels*, ce que reflètent les chiffres obtenus sur Google pour les deux traductions françaises proposées (3 occurrences au total pour les formes au singulier et au pluriel de *centre d'appel(s) au salaire minimum*), alors que l'anglais *minimum wage call center* en compte près de 2 500.

Tableau 11. Traduction française et rétrotraduction vers l'anglais du quintigramme *minimum wage call center fellow* dans la partie *Social Sciences* du Corpus de l'américain contemporain

Texte source	Traduction GT	Rétrotrad. GT	Traduction DL	Rétrotrad. DL
[...] that poor **minimum wage call center fellow** on the receiving end of your invective [...].	[...] ce pauvre **gars du centre d'appels au salaire minimum** qui reçoit vos invectives [...].	[...] that poor **guy <u>at</u> the minimum wage call center** who takes your name-calling [...].	[...] le pauvre **gars du centre d'appel au salaire minimum** qui reçoit vos invectives [...].	[...] the poor **guy <u>at</u> the minimum wage call center** who gets your invective [...].

L'exemple suivant implique un cas de figure dans lequel la longueur totale du GN pourrait avoir une influence sur l'absence de restitution de la prémodification à la rétrotraduction :

What PJ's is really saying is that they will have to pay <u>part of the cost</u> <u>**of**</u> <u>their</u> <u>**low wage workers health care**</u> instead of passing it on to Americans in their taxes.

On remarquera dans le Tableau 12 la quasi-similitude des traductions françaises, et la similitude parfaite des deux rétrotraductions, qui optent pour le même groupe prépositionnel (*for their low wage workers*). Notons au passage que l'orthographe standard du cas possessif anglais devrait théoriquement inclure une apostrophe (*low wage workers' health care*).

Tableau 12. Traduction française et rétrotraduction vers l'anglais du quintigramme *low wage workers health care* dans la partie *Social Sciences* du Corpus de l'américain contemporain

Texte source	Traduction GT	Rétrotrad. GT	Traduction DL	Rétrotrad. DL
[...] they will have to pay part of the cost of their **low wage workers health care** [...].	[...] ils devront payer une partie du coût des **soins de santé de leurs travailleurs à bas salaires** [...].	[...] they will have to pay some of the cost of **health care <u>for</u> their low-wage workers** [...].	[...] ils devront payer une partie du coût des **soins de santé de leurs travailleurs à bas salaire** [...].	[...] they will have to pay some of the cost of **health care <u>for</u> their low-wage workers** [...].

Le dernier cas que nous examinerons inclut une structure de génitif complexe :

> Employers' reliance on temporary staffing agencies is imperative for improving **[these and other low-wage workers'] health care access.**

Là encore, les deux traductions françaises sont quasi identiques, le choix du nombre pour *salaire(s)* étant d'ailleurs l'inverse de celui du Tableau 12 pour GT et DL. Tout comme dans l'exemple précédent, on observe une parfaite similitude des rétrotraductions (à l'exception de la variation *health care/healthcare*), avec la traduction par des groupes prépositionnels de « aux soins de santé » (*to health care*) et « de ces travailleurs » (*for these [...] workers*).

Tableau 13. Traduction française et rétrotraduction vers l'anglais du génitif *these and other low-wage workers' health care access* dans la partie *Social Sciences* du Corpus de l'américain contemporain

Texte source	Traduction GT	Rétrotrad. GT	Traduction DL	Rétrotrad. DL
[...] for improving these and other low-wage workers' health care access.	[...] pour améliorer l'accès aux soins de santé de ces travailleurs et d'autres travailleurs à bas salaire.	[...] to improving access to health care for these and other low-wage workers.	[...] pour améliorer l'accès aux soins de santé de ces travailleurs et d'autres travailleurs à bas salaires.	[...] to improve access to healthcare for these and other low-wage workers.

Les exemples des Tableaux 12 et 13 semblent indiquer qu'une augmentation de la longueur totale du groupe nominal pourrait être corrélée à une traduction littérale des groupes prépositionnels du français plutôt qu'à l'usage de la prémodification. Cette hypothèse demanderait cependant à être vérifiée par des études menées à plus grande échelle.

Conclusion

Les trigrammes nominaux de l'anglais qui sont lexicalisés (et qui sont également ceux dont la fréquence absolue est la plus élevée dans des corpus de référence tels que le Corpus de l'anglais américain) sont généralement traduits de manière stable et identique vers le français par les deux programmes de TA qui ont été comparés dans notre étude. On observe cependant une plus forte variation des résultats de la TA en langue de spécialité pour les trigrammes nominaux qui ne sont pas lexicalisés et dont la fréquence d'emploi est rare.

Le degré de variation est cependant supérieur lorsque les trigrammes ou quadrigrammes nominaux sont précédés par des adjectifs ou sont eux-mêmes des compléments à l'intérieur de groupes nominaux de taille élevée, notamment pour l'emploi de structures syntaxiques impliquant des cas possessifs. Par ailleurs, il ne semble pas y avoir d'avantage déterminant de l'un ou de l'autre des logiciels de TA dans le discours de l'économie. Cependant, on observe un léger avantage de DeepL par rapport à Google Translate pour ce qui concerne la restitution de la prémodification nominale utilisée dans la langue source lors des tests de rétrotraduction du français vers l'anglais. Quoi qu'il en soit, et en dépit des progrès récents de la TA neuronale en matière de fluidité, la traduction de l'espagnol ou du français vers l'anglais peut encore être améliorée, notamment en rendant plus compacts (*repacking*) les groupes nominaux complexes faisant intervenir la prémodification nominale.

Références

Davies, M. (2009). The 385+ million word corpus of contemporary American English (1990–2008+): Design, architecture, and linguistic insights. *International Journal of Corpus Linguistics*, 14(2): 159–190.

Gledhill, C. & Pecman, M. (2015). Cognitive packing and rhetorical packaging in English science writing: A comparative analysis of alternating pre-modified versus post-modified nominals. In *Colloque International de Linguistique GReG PLS IV;"Marqueurs et structures, quelles articulations dans la (re) construction du sens?"*.

Gledhill, C. & Pecman, M. (2018). On alternating pre- modified and post- modified nominals such as aspirin synthesis vs. synthesis of aspirin: Rhetorical and cognitive packing in English science writing. *Fachsprache- Journal of Professional and Scientific Communication*, 40(1+2): 24–46.

Maniez, F. (2017). An appraisal of recent breakthroughs in machine translation: The case of past participle-based compound adjectives in ESP. *ASp. la revue du GERAS*, 72: 29–48.

Tiedemann, J. & Scherrer, Y. (2017). Neural machine translation with extended context. In *Proceedings of the third workshop on discourse in machine translation, DISCOMT'17* (pp. 82–92). Copenhagen, Denmark. Association for Computational Linguistics.

Voita, E., Sennrich, R. & Titov, I. (2019). When a good translation is wrong in context: Context-aware machine translation improves on deixis, ellipsis, and lexical cohesion. *arXiv preprint arXiv:1905.05979*.

Ressources

Corpus, bases de données terminologiques et programmes de traduction en ligne

Corpus of Contemporary American English (COCA) : https://www.english-corpora.org/coca/

DeepL : https://www.deepl.com/translator

Google Translate : https://translate.google.fr/

Termium Plus : https://www.btb.termiumplus.gc.ca/

Darío Mantrana Gallego

5 Evaluation of economic-financial DE-ES translations: A comparative study between DeepL and Google Translate

The rise of new technologies has led to an increase in international economic activities and relations and, with them, the need for fast, accurate and high-quality economic translation. Technology does not only affect the field of economics; the field of translation is also seeing its impact. Neural machine translation (NMT) has progressed exponentially, presenting new challenges. In the field of economic-financial translation there are few studies on machine translation (MT). We therefore consider it relevant to study the quality of NMT engines with economic-financial texts. Below, we present a comparative study carried out with DeepL and Google Translate in order to analyse and evaluate German-Spanish translations of economic texts. The evaluations are carried out using the MQM framework and the metrics BLEU, chrF3 and TER. In this preliminary study, the errors committed by DeepL and Google Translate were identified and categorised in order to ascertain whether there are differences in translation quality between one engine and the other.

Introduction

Globalisation and technological progress bring with them a worldwide economic development and an intensification of international economic relations and activities. The translation industry has had to adapt to this rapid growth, the sheer scale of projects and the need for fast and effective communication. An example of the need for immediate translation can be seen in the European Commission, where a pilot machine translation (MT) project has been launched to translate press releases into all 24 official languages (Sorgi, 2023).

Professional translators have long been using computer-assisted translation tools: translation memories, search engines and terminology management and/or software to translate, revise and manage projects. However, the translation industry is facing a challenge that started around the 1950s. MT has been in development for several decades and today it is a booming technology that its use in some situations allows the professional translator to speed up the translation process and increase productivity (Läubli et al., 2019; Nunziatini, 2019; Rivera-Trigueros, 2022).

However, these translation technologies bring with them the need to create forms of quality assessment, which, like MT itself, are constantly being developed and improved. Neural machine translation (NMT) became a much better-known technology outside the research field in 2016, when a Google article was published announcing its new NMT system. The quality evaluations of their translations far outperformed all systems used thus far (Wu et al., 2016). NMT engines are becoming increasingly powerful and can achieve translations of surprisingly good quality. However, researchers are still looking for improvements and advances for MT to produce higher quality texts, as the quality of machine-generated translation cannot yet match that of the professional (Toral et al., 2018; Läubli et al., 2018, 2020, Läubli, 2022) and it is still necessary for the human translator to make some corrections at a linguistic and cultural level to better adapt the translation to the target audience. Furthermore, Castilho et al. (2017: 118) and Way (2018: 16) agree and state that MT quality still requires post-editing.

When assessing the quality of translations, it is important to bear in mind that factors such as purpose, target audience or the criteria of the professional evaluator are not the only ones that affect the quality of MT. Other factors, such as the type of MT engine, its level of training, the internal structure, the language combination, the subject matter of the text or the degree of specialisation, play a part.

Presently, we submit comparative study carried out with DeepL, an NMT engine launched in 2017, and Google Translate, an NMT engine launched in 2016. The main objectives are to analyse and evaluate the translations from German into Spanish of economic-financial text fragments using the MQM framework and the automatic metrics BLEU, chrF3 and TER. The aim is to observe whether there are differences between the translations of the two NMT engines. To this end, the errors made by DeepL and Google Translate in a series of specialised texts have been detected and analysed. MutNMT (https://ntradumatica.uab.cat/), an open-source platform that evaluates NMT, was used for the automatic evaluation.

The following section elaborates on the methodology employed in this study. Sections three and four set out the results of the manual and automatic evaluations respectively, and the last section develops conclusions and names ideas for future research.

Methodology

For this analysis, a small corpus of 100 segments using the language combination German-Spanish has been compiled. The corpus under study are economic- financial texts with a medium- high degree of specialisation. The texts compiled for this corpus come from the publications, reports, speeches and press releases of the European Central Bank and from texts collected from economic and financial websites, such as rechnungswesen-verstehen.de or gesetze-im-internet.de, and from texts worked on during further training courses, which were translated by the researcher himself. The texts deal with different topics such as types of contracts, regulatory frameworks, banking operations, types of taxes, documentary credits, financial assets, foreign trade, stock exchange and international economic transactions, among others.

As mentioned before, the NMT engines chosen are DeepL and Google Translate. While Google Translate was launched in 2006 as a statistics-based machine translation engine, it was not until 2016 that it became an NMT engine. Both engines are free online machine translation tools and can translate a large number of languages.

Once the corpus and the NMT engines were defined, we established the evaluation methods to be used in this comparative study. There are two ways of evaluating MT quality: manual evaluation and automatic evaluation. While manual evaluation is carried out by a human professional, automatic evaluation is carried out by an algorithm. The machine translation outputs in this study have been evaluated both manually and automatically.

Manual and automatic quality evaluation

For the manual quality evaluation, we used the classification presented by the MQM framework (Multidimensional Quality Metrics), developed by the German Research Centre for Artificial Intelligence (*Deutsches*

Forschungszentrum für Künstliche Intelligenz) under the framework of the European project QTLaunchPad. The MQM framework does not provide a metric per se, however offers the user a flexible framework to customise and define evaluation metrics that are adapted to the evaluation criteria and specifications of the study to be developed (Lommel et al., 2015). It is worth mentioning the functional approach of this model insofar as translation quality depends on the communication objective and the context (Burchardt et al., 2016: 37).

This comprehensive quality assessment model proposes more than 100 types of problems and is divided into eight main categories (dimensions) which, in turn, are broken down into several subcategories (issues), which are further subdivided into more categories (Lommel et al., 2015). It also defines four degrees of error penalties, scoring critical, major, minor and neutral errors with 100, 10, 1 or 0 points, respectively (Sánchez Ramos & Rico Pérez, 2020: 38). The most serious errors are those that cause the translation to fail to meet its purpose and ergo cannot be used. Major errors prevent the content from being properly understood, minor errors sometimes go unnoticed by the end user and do not affect the content of the text and, finally, unimportant or null errors are annotations by the evaluators to make changes, but they do not count as errors as such and are therefore not penalised (Lommel 2018: 120–121).

We followed the guidelines proposed by Lommel (2018) to adapt the MQM framework to our context. We adopted the analytical approach to identify and categorise text problems in greater detail (Lommel et al., 2015). We also defined the evaluation specifications for the translations, i.e. the values assigned to the parameters of the MQM framework. As a next step in the analysis, we chose two of the eleven parameters: target audience and purpose of the translation, even though texts chosen for the corpus have a medium-high degree of specialisation, they should nonetheless be understandable for both experts and laypersons who need information on these topics.

Taking the above parameters into account, this study focuses on three of the eight categories defined by the MQM framework: accuracy, fluency and terminology, given that we consider these to be the most relevant aspects in the context of economic and financial translation. As we worked with a small corpus, we decided to break down only the accuracy category into the following: mistranslation, omission and addition. For the purposes of the category's fluency and terminology, we did not break them down into subcategories. Table 1 presents the chosen categories and subcategories in a more visual form:

Table 1. Selection of categories and subcategories for the analysis

Accuracy	
	Addition
	Mistranslation
	Omission
Fluency	
Terminology	

While evaluating MT results manually is an activity that requires the work of a professional and involves costs, time and subjectivity, it does however allow for a thorough analysis of every translation detail and error (Panic, 2020).

To eliminate financial, time and subjectivity issues, automatic MT evaluation metrics such as BLEU, chrF3 and TER were developed to replace the human professional with an algorithm that works using human translations as reference text. However, these also have limitations (Way, 2018). They do not take into account the source text and only compare the frequency of phrases or words between the MT-translated text and the reference translation. These three automatic metrics are used, as they are the ones computed by the pedagogically-oriented MutNMT platform.

The BLEU (Bilingual Evaluation Understudy) metric was presented in 2002 by Papineni et al. as a "method of automatic machine translation evaluation that is quick, inexpensive, and language-independent that correlates highly with human evaluation, and that has little marginal cost per run" (Papineni et al., 2002: 1). BLEU calculates MT accuracy by comparing the text produced by the engine with reference translations generated by human translators. This algorithm measures the number of word-level n-grams that match in the MT and the reference translation (Papineni et al., 2002) it then calculates a weighted average. The more n-grams match the reference translation, the higher the score the MT receives. The most relevant factors that BLEU uses to calculate the score are: translation length, translated words and word order (Shterionov et al., 2018: 222). The chrF3 metric (Popovic, 2015) also calculates the number of n-grams that match the reference translation, that said, unlike BLEU, it is measured at the character level. Both BLEU and chrF3 scores range from 0 to 100, with higher scores indicating better MT quality. This evaluation metric operates "at character-level with a higher correlation with human judgments than BLEU" (Marie, 2022: 2). The last machine evaluation metric, TER (Translation Error Rate), measures the percentage of characters that the translator must correct to match the reference translation (Snover et al., 2006). The lower the number of edits, the better the MT result (Shterionov et al., 2018: 222).

The automatic evaluation is carried out on the MutNMT platform, a web application developed under the framework of the MultitraiNMT Erasmus+ project. This platform offers a wide range of functions including corpus and NMT engine library, NMT engine training, machine translation, output inspection and automatic evaluation (Forcada et al., 2022). The automatic evaluation function allows the user to upload their own .txt files and the platform directly calculates the results for the BLEU, chrF3 and TER metrics.

Once the automatic evaluation metrics and the manual metrics (with specifications, analysis type, parameters, dimensions and different error categories) are set, we then perform the analysis of the translated segments.

Manual evaluation and results

In this study, a total of 100 segments have been analysed, with each segment containing an average of 15–20 words (source text). As shown in Table 2, Google Translate had a total of 8 fewer errors than DeepL in the manual evaluation. In all the analysed categories, Google Translate performed better, even though the difference is small.

Table 2. Results of the manual evaluation

Category		Deepl	Google Translate
Terminology		39	37
Fluency		4	3
Accuracy		31	25
	Mistranslation	28	22
	Omission	3	3
	Addition	0	0
TOTAL		74	65

We can ascertain that most of the errors produced by both DeepL and Google Translate are terminology and accuracy errors. The following table (Table 3) shows some examples of terminology errors (in bold). We also find some examples in which DeepL makes some terminology errors (2) and (4), but Google Translate resolves the translation correctly. In contrast, there are also examples, in which DeepL's output is correct, but Google Translate commits a terminological mistake (5).

Based on the total number of errors, we can establish that 52.70 % (DeepL) and 56.9 % (Google Translate) of all errors belong to this category. Furthermore, it is of significant importance to mention that in some segments we have found terminological instability, since the engines sometimes mistranslated a term, only to find that the same term had been translated correctly or nonsensically in other analysed segments. An example of this is the term "Vorleistungen" (3), DeepL translated it as "consumos intermedios" and as "insumos intermedios", the second translation being correct, and Google Translate translated it as "trabajo preliminar" and as "consumo intermedio". Another term showing terminological instability is "bedeutende Institute" (1, 2) translated by DeepL as "principales instituciones" or "intermediarios financieros" and translated by Google Translate as "SI" and "entidades significativas", only the latter term being correct.

Table 3. Terminology errors

	Source Text	Reference Text	DeepL	Google Translate
1	Insbesondere **SIs** haben insgesamt ihr Engagement in gehebelten Transaktionen in den letzten Jahren deutlich erhöht.	En particular, las **entidades significativas** han incrementado sustancialmente su exposición a las operaciones apalancadas en los últimos años.	Los **intermediarios financieros**, en particular, han aumentado considerablemente su exposición global a las operaciones apalancadas en los últimos años.	Los **SI** en particular han aumentado su exposición a las transacciones apalancadas en general en los últimos años.
2	**Bedeutende Institute** weiterhin mit soliden Kapital- und Liquiditätspositionen.	Las **entidades significativas** mantienen posiciones de capital y de liquidez sólidas.	Las **principales instituciones** siguen teniendo una sólida posición de capital y liquidez.	Las entidades significativas siguen manteniendo posiciones sólidas de capital y liquidez.
3	Berechnung: Summe aller Produktionen abzüglich aller **Vorleistungen.**	Cálculo: suma de todalaproducción menos todo el conjunto del **insumo.**	Cálculo: suma de toda la producción menos todos los **consumos intermedios.**	Cálculo: suma de todas las producciones menos todo el **trabajo preliminar.**
4	Der **Bürge** verpflichtet sich gegenüber dem Gläubiger einer dritten Person, für die Erfüllung der Verbindlichkeiten des Dritten einzustehen.	El **fiador** se compromete con el acreedor de una tercera persona a garantizar el cumplimiento de las deudas del tercero.	El **avalista** se compromete ante el acreedor de un tercero a garantizar el cumplimiento de las obligaciones de éste.	El fiador se obliga frente al acreedor de un tercero a ser responsable del cumplimiento de las obligaciones del tercero.
5	Auch, wenn die Namen ähnlich klingen: Der Dienstvertrag ist nicht mit dem **Werkvertrag** zu verwechseln.	Aunque los nombres suenen parecidos, no se debe confundir un contrato de servicios con un **contrato de obra.**	Aunque los nombres suenen parecidos: el contratodeservicios nodebeconfundirse con el contrato de obra.	Aunque los nombres suenen parecidos: El contratodeservicios no debe confundirse con el **contrato de trabajo.**

Within the accuracy dimension, the largest number of errors belong to the mistranslation subcategory. One of the difficulties of MQM evaluation is the fine line between mistranslation and terminology errors. According to the MQM error typology, mistranslations are defined as "target content that does not accurately represent the source content" (Lommel et al., 2022) and terminology errors are "errors that arise when a term does not conform to the normative terminology standards of the domain or organisation or when a term in the target text is not the correct normative equivalent of the corresponding term in the source text" (Lommel et al., 2022). In our study, all financial or economic terms that were mistranslated were categorised as terminology errors, as we concurred the NMT engine selected the wrong term. Other words or phrases translated inappropriately were categorised as mistranslation. Table 4 presents examples of the accuracy errors (in bold) made by the two NMT engines.

For the purposes of our study, the accuracy dimension is divided into three major subcategories: mistranslation, omission and addition. Under the subcategory of mistranslation, we have also analysed ambiguous translation, false friends, overly literal translations and translations that should not have been translated. The first example (1) in Table 4 refers to the category of mistranslation. The second (2) is a clear example of overly literal translation. The following segments (3, 4) are examples of ambiguous translation and omission, respectively. Neither addition nor false friend errors were found in any of the analysed segments. Accuracy errors account for 41.8 % (DeepL) and 38.4 % (Google Translate) of the total amount of errors found in the evaluation.

Table 4. Accuracy errors

	Source Text	Reference Text	DeepL	Google Translate
1	**Im Unterschied zur** Schweizer Börse lagen sie am Dienstag noch im roten Bereich.	**A diferencia de** la bolsa suiza, seguían en números rojos el martes.	**Por el contrario,** la bolsa suiza seguía en números rojos el martes.	A diferencia de la bolsa de valores suiza, todavía estaban en números rojos el martes.
2	Damit ist dieser Wirtschaftssektor **"material- und kapitalintensiv"**.	Este sector económico demanda gran cantidad de recursos naturales e inversiones dinerarias.	Esto hace que este sector de la economía sea **"intensivo en materiales y capital"**.	Este sector económico es "intensivo en materiales y capital".
3	Um den Bürgen vor unüberlegten Zusagen zu schützen, **schreibt** das Gesetz **für die Bürgschaftserklärung die Schriftform vor.**	Para proteger al fiador de promesas realizadas irreflexivamente, la ley **exige la declaración del fiador por escrito.**	Para proteger al avalista de promesas precipitadas, la ley exige **la forma escrita de la declaración de garantía.**	Para proteger al fiador de promesas imprudentes, la ley establece que la declaración de garantía debe constar por escrito.
4	Dieser Steuer wird allerdings nur vom Nettovermögen – Bruttovermögen abzüglich der **evtl.** vorhandenen Schulden erhoben.	Sin embargo, este impuesto solo grava el patrimonio neto, es decir, el patrimonio bruto menos las **posibles** deudas existentes.	Sin embargo, este impuesto sólo grava el patrimonio neto, es decir, el patrimonio bruto menos las deudas.	Sin embargo, este impuesto solo se aplica a los activos netos: los activos brutos menos las deudas existentes.

Only 5.41 % (DeepL) and 4.61 % (Google Translate) of the errors found are fluency errors and the vast majority are incorrectly used prepositions and some incorrect wrong verb tenses. Based on the reference translations, there were very few segments with incorrect punctuation.

In some segments it is evident that the engines completely change the meaning of the text or make it unintelligible, as shown in the examples in Table 5. We have marked these errors (in bold) as serious errors and penalised them with 100 points each, as indicated by the MQM framework.

Tabla 5. Critical errors

	Source Text	Reference Text	DeepL	Google Translate
1	**Im Unterschied zur** Schweizer Börse lagen sie am Dienstag noch im roten Bereich.	**A diferencia de** la bolsa suiza, seguían en números rojos el martes.	**Por el contrario,** la bolsa suiza seguía en números rojos el martes.	A diferencia de la bolsa de valores suiza, todavía estaban en números rojos el martes.
2	Demnach haben die EZB und die Europäische Kommission dem Rat der Europäischen Union mindestens alle zwei Jahre oder auf Antrag eines EU-Mitgliedstaats, für den eine Ausnahmeregelung gilt, zu berichten, **„inwieweit die Mitgliedstaaten, für die eine Ausnahmeregelung gilt, bei der Verwirklichung der Wirtschafts- und Währungsunion ihren Verpflichtungen bereits nachgekommen sind“.**	De conformidad con este artículo, una vez cada dos años como mínimo, o a petición de cualquier Estado miembro de la UE acogido a una excepción, el BCE y la Comisión Europea presentarán informes al Consejo de la UE **«acerca de los avances que hayan realizado los Estados miembros acogidos a una excepción en el cumplimiento de sus obligaciones en relación con la realización de la unión económica y monetaria».**	Según esta disposición, el BCE y la Comisión Europea deben informar al Consejo de la Unión Europea al menos cada dos años, o a petición de un Estado miembro de la UE acogido a una excepción, "sobre la medida en que los Estados miembros acogidos a una excepción han cumplido ya sus obligaciones en relación con la realización de la unión económica y monetaria".	Según esto, el BCE y la Comisión Europea tienen que informar al Consejo de la Unión Europea al menos cada dos años o a petición de un Estado miembro de la UE con una excepción, **"en qué medida los Estados miembros con una excepción aplican en realización de la economía- y la Unión Monetaria ya han cumplido sus obligaciones".**

(*continued on next page*)

Table 5. Continued

	Source Text	Reference Text	DeepL	Google Translate
3	Die EZB verwendet die **BCBS-239-Grundsätze** als Richtschur für ihre laufende Aufsichtstätigkeit zur Bewertung der Risikodaten-Aggregationskapazitäten und der Verfahren zur Risikoberichterstattung der Institute.	En el marco de sus actividades ordinarias de supervisión, el BCE utiliza los **principios recogidos** en BCBS 239 como referencia para evaluar la capacidad de agregación de datos de riesgos y las prácticas de presentación de información sobre riesgos de las entidades de crédito.	El BCE utiliza los **239 Principios** del BCBS como guía para sus actividades de supervisión en curso a fin de evaluar la capacidad de agregación de datos sobre riesgos y los procesos de información sobre riesgos de las entidades.	El BCE utiliza los principios BCBS 239 para guiar su trabajo de supervisión en curso para evaluar las capacidades de agregación de datos de riesgo y los procesos de información de riesgo de las entidades.

On the other hand, it is also noteworthy that, although in some of the segments analysed there were up to three different types of errors, we also found segments without errors, such as the examples set forth in Table 6. These segments do not present problems of fluency or accuracy and the terminology used is also correct.

Table 6. No errors

	Source Text	Reference Text	DeepL	Google Translate
1	Um den Stand der wirtschaftlichen Konvergenz in den EU-Mitgliedstaaten zu prüfen, die den Euro einführen wollen, verwendet die EZB ein einheitliches Analyseschema.	Para evaluar la situación de la convergencia económica de los Estados miembros de la UE que aspiran a adoptar el euro, el BCE utiliza un marco común de análisis.	Para evaluar el estado de la convergencia económica en los Estados miembros de la UE que desean adoptar el euro, el BCE utiliza un marco analítico común.	Para examinar el estado de la convergencia económica en los Estados miembros de la UE que planean adoptar el euro, el BCE utiliza un esquema de análisis común.

Table 6. Continued

	Source Text	Reference Text	DeepL	Google Translate
2	Die Wirtschaftsentwicklung wird daher in den betreffenden Ländern im Rückblick betrachtet, wobei prinzipiell die vergangenen zehn Jahre einbezogen werden.	A este respecto, la evolución económica de los países se examina con un enfoque retrospectivo que cubre, en principio, los diez últimos años.	Por tanto, el desarrollo económico de los países en cuestión se analiza retrospectivamente, incluyendo en principio los últimos diez años.	Por lo tanto, el desarrollo económico de los países en cuestión se examina retrospectivamente, y en principio se incluyen los últimos diez años.
3	Für die Banken, die dem parallelen SSM-Stresstest unterzogen werden, veröffentlicht die EZB aggregierte Ergebnisse und ausgewählte bankspezifische Informationen.	Para las entidades que participen en la prueba de resistencia paralela del MUS, el BCE publicará los resultados agregados y una selección de información específica de cada entidad.	En el caso de los bancos sujetos a la prueba de resistencia paralela del MUS, el BCE publica los resultados agregados e información seleccionada específica de cada banco.	Para los bancos que están sujetos a la prueba de resistencia paralela del MUS, el BCE publica resultados agregados e información seleccionada específica del banco.
4	Die überraschend positive Entwicklung im vierten Quartal 2022 ging zwar vor allem auf schwächere Importe zurück und deutete nicht unbedingt auf eine stärkere zugrunde liegende Wachstumsdynamik hin, doch trugen die verbesserten Aussichten für die Energieversorgung und die Preisentwicklung dazu bei, dass die Unsicherheit zum Ende des Quartals abnahm.	Aunque la evolución más positiva de lo previsto observada en el cuarto trimestre de 2022 reflejó, en gran medida, el debilitamiento de las importaciones y, por tanto, no sugiere necesariamente un mayor dinamismo subyacente del crecimiento, la mejora de las perspectivas de la oferta y los precios de la energía contribuyó a una disminución de la incertidumbre hacia finales del trimestre.	Aunque la evolución sorprendentemente positiva del cuarto trimestre de 2022 se debió principalmente al debilitamiento de las importaciones y no apuntó necesariamente a un mayor impulso del crecimiento subyacente, la mejora de las perspectivas de la oferta energética y la evolución de los precios contribuyeron a reducir la incertidumbre al final del trimestre.	Si bien el desempeño mejor de lo esperado en el cuarto trimestre de 2022 fue impulsado principalmente por importaciones más débiles y no necesariamente apuntó a un mayor impulso de crecimiento subyacente, la mejora de las perspectivas para el suministro de energía y la evolución de los precios ayudó a reducir la incertidumbre hacia el final del trimestre.

Although there is a small difference between the number of errors made by DeepL and those made by Google Translate, they both came out with almost the same result in the quality analysis. For this calculation, errors were penalised according to the MQM framework and the following formula was applied: Score = 1 – (Penalties/WordCount) (Lommel, 2018: 122).

The result obtained in our analysis is 0.56 (DeepL) and 0.59 (Google Translate), which expressed as a percentage is 56.7 % for DeepL and 59.4 % for Google Translate. While it is true that Google Translate made fewer numbers of errors in the analysis, the final results do not differ much from each other since, although some segments contained different types of errors in each engine, the severity and the level of penalties were similar. According to Lommel (2018: 122), it depends on the evaluation arrangement and the evaluators the minimum score a translation needs to be considered acceptable.

Automatic evaluation and results

The same corpus of 100 segments was used for the automatic evaluation and, as mentioned above, it was carried out on the MutNMT platform. The results obtained by the NMT engines are presented in the following table (Table 7):

Table 7. Automatic evaluation results

	DeepL	Google Translate
BLEU	46	33.9
chrF3	66.54	59.43
TER	50.33	68.83

The score obtained by DeepL with the BLEU metric is higher than the score obtained by Google Translate. According to this metric, on a scale of 1 to 100, the higher the percentage, the better the translation quality of the engine. The chrF3 metric gave 66.54 and 59.43 for DeepL and Google Translate, respectively. Like BLEU, the higher the score obtained in this metric, the better the MT quality. Finally, DeepL also scores better on the TER metric, as it requires 50.33 % changes, while Google Translate requires 68.83 % modification.

In this comparative study, we are pleasantly surprised by the results obtained in both manual and automatic evaluation, however, we believe that these NMT engines still do not reach the quality levels required for economic-financial translation and should be combined with pre-editing and/or post-editing, in order to be a useful resource that improves the performance and productivity of the professional translator.

Conclusions and future research

In this study, the objectives were to analyse and evaluate manually and automatically the quality of translations of different economic-financial fragments from German into Spanish and to observe the differences between the NMT engines of DeepL and Google Translate. The translation quality results show that, although the engines output is quite good in some translations, it is not enough to translate this type of texts and requires pre-editing or post-editing. We agree with Forcada (2017: 13) that, although the translations may be fluent as a read text, they may contain content errors, as we have observed.

In our case, both DeepL and Google Translate make significant and some serious translation errors that require post-editing. With regard to the second objective, it is evident that the engines make different errors and that the results obtained also differ. In the manual evaluation Google Translate scored better than DeepL, although the margin was minimal – only a few hundredths of a point (or 3 % difference). In contrast, the automatic evaluation proves the opposite and DeepL scores better. In this evaluation, the difference between the results is more noticeable, however, the results are not too far apart. The fact that one engine scores better in one analysis and the other engine in the other is not too remarkable, as the results are average and do not stand out as either great results or disastrous translations. On the one hand, we know that manual evaluation is time-consuming and the subjectivity factor is impossible to eliminate, even if all the evaluation parameters and agreements have been set to minimise this, the quality criteria are different and vary according to the evaluator. We have also noted the limitations of automatic metrics, as they do not take into account the source text, meaning and intentionality, but rather only compare characters/words/phrases that match the reference human translation. For these reasons, we decided to perform both types of translation quality assessment in order to obtain the most accurate results possible.

We are satisfied with both the scoring following the MQM metric and the scoring of BLEU, chrF3 and TER consider that some segments contained apt and valid translations and that some of the translation proposals generated were interesting, however, for this study and this text typology, they do not reach the "acceptable" level and post-editing of the texts translated by the engines is required. Despite all this, we must also bear in mind that both DeepL and Google Translate NMT engines are so accessible to everyone, however, we do not have access to their internal structure and they are not trained solely for economic-financial translations with the German-Spanish language pair.

It should also be mentioned that the study corpus is small and limited. In the near future, the idea is to extend the scope of this corpus and to test the results on a larger scale. Moreover, following the line of specialised text translation, our future research will focus on comparative studies with other NMT engines. Likewise, it would be interesting to analyse whether, in the future, the translations of the segments analysed in this study improve.

Bibliography

Burchardt, A., Harris, K., Rehm, G. & Uszkoreit, H. (2016). Towards a systematic and human-informed paradigm for high-quality machine translation. In *Proceedings of the LREC 2016 workshop "Translation Evaluation – From Fragmented Tools and Data Sets to an Integrated Ecosystem"* (pp. 35–42). European Language Resources Association (ELRA), http://www.cracking-the-language-barrier.eu/mt-eval-workshop-2016/

Castilho, S., Moorkens, J., Gaspari, F., Calixto, J., Tinsley, J. & Way, A. (2017). Is neural machine translation the new state of the art? *The Prague Bulletin of Mathematical Linguistics*, 108: 109–120.

Forcada, M. (2017). *Making sense of neural machine translation.* https://www.dlsi.ua.es/~mlf/docum/forcada17j2.pdf

Forcada, M., Sánchez-Gijón, P., Kenny, D., Sánchez-Martínez, F., Pérez Ortiz, J., Superbo, R., Ramírez Sánchez, G., Torres-Hostench, O. & Rossi, C. (2022). MultitraiNMT Erasmus+ project: Machine Translation Training for multilingual citizens (multitrainmt.eu). In *Proceedings of the 23rd annual conference of the European association for machine translation* (pp. 291–292), Ghent, Belgium: European Association for Machine Translation.

Läubli, S. (2022). *Wie unterscheidet sich die Qualität von maschineller Übersetzung von professioneller Humanübersetzung?* [Conference presentation]. ASTT-Tagung 2022: Eine Welt ohne Babel?, Germersheim, Germany.

Läubli, S., Amrhein, C., Düggelin, P., Gonzalez, B., Zwahlen, A. & Volk, M. (2019). Post-editing productivity with neural machine translation: An empirical assessment of speed and quality in the banking and finance domain. In *Proceedings of machine translation summit XVII: Research track* (pp. 267–272).

Läubli, S., Castilho, S., Neubig, G., Sennrich, R., Shen, Q. & Toral, A. (2020). A set of recommendations for assessing human–machine parity in language translation. *Journal of Artificial Intelligence Research*, 67: 653–672.

Läubli, S., Sennrich, R. & Volk, M. (2018). Has machine translat tion achieved human parity? a case for document- level evaluation. In *Proceedings of the 2018 Conference on Empirical Methods in Natural Language Processing* (pp. 4791–4796). https://aclanthology.org/D18-1512/

Lommel, A. (2018). Metrics for translation quality assessment: A case for standardising error typologies. In J. Moorkens, S. Castilho, F. Gaspari & S. Doherty (Eds.), *Translation quality assessment. Machine translation: Technologies and applications* (pp. 109–127). Springer.

Lommel, A., Burchardt, A. & Uszkoreit, H. (2015). *Multidimensional Quality Metrics (MQM) definition.* https://www.qt21.eu/mqm-definition/definition-2015-12-30.html

Lommel, A., Burchardt, A., Görög, A., Uszkoreit, H. & Melby, A. (2022). *MQM core typology*. https://themqm.info/typology/

Marie, B. (2022). *An automatic evaluation of the WMT22 general machine translation task*.

Nunziatini, M. (2019). Machine translation in the financial services industry: A case study. In *Proceedings of machine translation summit XVII: Translator, project and user tracks*, 2, 57–63.

Panic, M. (2020). *Implementation of machine translation: What to consider?* TAUS. Retrieved 9th July 2022, from https://www.taus.net/resources/blog/implementation-of-machine-translation-what-to-consider

Papineni, K., Roukos, S., Ward, T. & Zhu, W. (2002). Bleu: A method for automatic evaluation of machine translation. In *Proceedings of the 40th annual meeting of the association for computational linguistics* (pp. 311–318).

Popovic, M. (2015). chrF: Character n-gram F-score for automatic MT evaluation. In *Proceedings of the tenth workshop on statistical machine translation* (pp. 392–395).

Sánchez Ramos, M. & Rico Pérez, C. (2020). *Traducción automática. Conceptos clave, procesos de evaluación y técnicas de posedición.* Comares.

Shterionov, D., Superbo, R., Nagle, P., Casanellas, L., O'dowd, T. & Way, A. (2018). Human versus automatic quality evaluation of NMT and PBSMT. *Machine Translation*, 32(3): 217–235.

Snover, M., Dorr, B., Schwartz, R., Micciulla, L. & Makhoul, J. (2006). A study of translation edit rate with targeted human annotation. In *Proceedings of the 7th conference of the association for machine translation in the Americas: Technical papers* (pp. 223–231).

Sorgi, G. (2023, June 15). EU gives more power to AI translation machines. *POLITICO*. https://www.politico.eu/article/ai-technology-eu-commission-parliament-gives-more-power-to-ai-translation-machines/

Rivera-Trigueros, I. (2022). Machine translation systems and quality assessment: A systematic review. In *Language Resources & Evaluation*, 56, 593–619.

Toral, A., Castilho, S., Hu, K. & Way, A. (2018). Attaining the unattainable? Reassessing claims of human parity in neural machine translation. In *Proceedings of the third conference on machine translation: Research papers* (pp. 113–123). https://aclanthology.org/W18-6312/

Way, A. (2018). Quality expectations of machine translation. In J. Moorkens, S. Castilho, F. Gaspari & S. Doherty (Eds.), *Translation quality assessment* (pp. 159–178). Springer.

Wu, Y., Schuster, M., Chen, Z., Quoc, V., Norouzi, M., Macherey, W., Krikun, M., Cao, Y., Gao, Q., Macherey, K., Klingner, J., Shah, A., Johnson, M., Liu, X., Kaiser, L., Gouws, S., Kato, Y., Kudo, T., Kazawa, H., & Dean, J. (2016). *Google's neural machine translation system: Bridging the gap between human and machine translation.* https://arxiv.org/abs/1609.08144

Éric Poirier

6 Essential resources of Canadian origin in economic and financial translation for practising, teaching, learning and research purposes

This paper aims to explore the field of economic and financial translation in Canada and describe different types of resources made in Canada that contribute to the development of specialization in translation, in teaching and learning translation and in the advances in this specialized field of knowledge. By suggesting information resources and datasets, the paper is also interested into the future of the field and suggests different ways that information and datasets from Canadian origin may contribute to corpus-based translation studies in economy and finance and to the teaching and learning of specialized translation in economy and finance. It will describe primary, secondary, and tertiary resources available for financial translation and present four Canadian examples of these resources that can be of help in the development of specialized translation, in teaching and learning translation and in the advances in this specialized field of knowledge. This paper is targeting international audiences that are interested in the works of Canadian origin in the field of economic and financial translation. The survey of resources, datasets and information of Canadian origin is not exhaustive. The emphasis is on the most important resources from the point of view of the author who is a professional translator and university teacher specialized in finance and economy.

Introduction

In Canada, as elsewhere, and given the rapidly growing demand for translation, the need for translation services specialized in economics and finance is not about to diminish. The statement made by our colleague Daniel Gallego-Hernandez (2014: 15) regarding the situation in Spain, according to which training and documentary resources in this field of translation specialization were insufficient at the time in Spain, has not lost its relevance today with regard to the situation in Canada.

The purpose of this paper is to first present a brief overview of four of the most important and crucial primary, secondary and tertiary resources from Canadian authors or organizations that have influenced the teaching and practice of economic and financial translation in Canada, and more specifically in Québec in the translation from English to French. And second, to describe some datasets and text-based resources that can contribute to the advances in specialized translation and corpus-based translation studies specialized in economy and finance.

Part I: Crucial resources of Canadian origin for specialized translation or teaching and learning economic and financial translation

In the first part below I present an overview of most important resources in economic and financial translation. This first part is divided in five sections.

Categorizing documentation materials for translation purposes

When it comes to presenting and analysing specialized materials used for translation in finance, business and economics, as well as for any documents used for the purpose of non-specialized translation, I categorize documents into three types based on their unique role in translation. This categorization draws upon the traditional classification of information sources as primary, secondary, and tertiary materials in documentation, research, and Library science. I have adapted this typology for translation operations using different sources of information, starting with translated texts found in parallel corpora. In translation, authentic primary sources encompass linguistic corpora, while other reference documents are categorized as secondary sources. Bilingual or monolingual dictionaries, glossaries, vocabularies, and similar reference materials, despite not explicitly citing the origin of the translations they provide, are deemed primary resources due to their direct utilization by translators in the translation process. Though these resources commonly rely on unilingual or bilingual (parallel) corpora or even other dictionaries, their status as primary sources in translation remains intact. Concerning terminological databases, they are deemed secondary resources because they consistently acknowledge and cite their sources, despite their frequent use as bilingual dictionaries, typically regarded as primary sources in the realm of translation. Terminological databases also offer valuable insights and comments on the application of certain expressions for precise translation purposes, providing an additional rationale for categorizing these works as secondary sources.

Primary resources are directly involved in the translation process, they offer translation solutions or meaning definitions of source language-culture words, expressions or terms. These resources typically include general and specialized bilingual dictionaries, glossaries and vocabularies as well as monolingual resources such as language dictionaries as well as thesauruses and synonym dictionaries. In this last case, synonym dictionaries suggest intralingual equivalences which can be very handy in order to find the *mot juste* in target language. As regards the training of translators, the adequate use of these resources is crucial to the success of learning how to translate. For example, one important element of knowledge when consulting these materials is to never forget that the most common translation solution, often firstly provided in the document, is not necessarily the best one in the translation to be done. Some contextual choices (before and after this lexical element) and meaning discrimination based on discourse situation may point to other more relevant secondary translation solutions.

Secondary resources play an indirect yet significant role in the translation process, influencing the reasoning and decision-making process leading to the selection of a final translation solution by the translator. These resources commonly encompass columns and sections within newsletters specially designed for translators. Additionally, they encompass a wide array of specific materials and documents, or segments thereof, offering encyclopedic information, including observations and explanations related to specialized concepts or activities. Reviews, analyses, and comparisons of translation solutions also fall under the category of secondary materials, as they actively contribute to the enhancement of reasoning capabilities and knowledge development for translators.

Tertiary resources function as comprehensive compilations, aggregating both primary and secondary resources into unified collections. Due to their presentation as lists of primary or secondary resources, they are often overlooked as distinct entities. In the context of specialized translation, tertiary documentation may also consist of complete documents providing exhaustive documentation or comprehensive courses on translation or specific areas within the specialized field. Such resources encompass information resource integrators, which furnish multiple links or documents that prove beneficial in facilitating the translation process, as well as specialized translation textbooks tailored for distinct areas within the field of translation specialization. An exemplar of these integrators can be found in the reference materials listed at the conclusion of textbooks or individual chapters.

Essential primary resources in financial translation from Canada

Some interesting primary resources of Canadian origin deserves the attention of an international audience. One of these resources is the famous Lexique de cooccurrents from Betty Cohen which was first published in 1986 and re-edited in 2011 at Linguatech Editor, and more recently in 2023 at Presses de l'Université de Montréal which bought the entire catalogue of Linguatech in 2022. What is very interesting (and language neutral) about this book is that it uses the concept of lexical function (Mel'čuk, 1996) from the meaning-text theory framework as applied to the area of stock exchange and economic analysis in French. In practice it focuses on the very general axis of growth/decline which serves as categorization of collocations. For example, for the entry crise (crisis), we find these collocations (among others): **Start:** éclater (the crisis erupts, beaks out); **growth:** s'aggraver (the crisis deepens, worsens); **neutral:** affecter, toucher (the crisis affects, hits); **decline:** facing (up) the crisis, coping with the crisis; **end:** disparaître, résorber (disappears, vanishes, is easing, subsiding); **others:** être en crise (to be in crisis). The element in bold are descriptors used for all the collocations provided in the book (our translation since the book provides only French collocations). This book is not freely available on-line but may be purchased on-line from the publisher (now Presses de l'Université de Montréal). I have published a review of the second edition of the book in *Circuit Magazine* (Poirier, 2012) that is available on-line (https://www.circuitmagazine.org/archives).

Inspired by the idea of Jean-François Joly, former director of the former CICA (Canadian Institute of Chartered Accountant), which is now CPA (Chartered Professional Accountants) Québec organization, another innovative work from Louis Ménard and Antoni Dandonneau (2009) is available freely on-line and is the result of a major collaborative team of linguists, translators and specialists in accounting, law and management. This primary resource is called Dictionary of Derivatives and Other Financial Instruments = Dictionnaire des dérivés et autres instruments financiers and it offers investors, financial industry professionals, translators and the general public a bilingual (English and French) reference covering concepts that can seem complex and confusing in specific and specialized market exchange instruments. The terms are all defined in English and in French and are all freely available in electronic format by selecting the option View all terms in the homepage. I have also published a review of this dictionary in Circuit magazine (Poirier, 2010) that is available on-line.

Another very important English-French dictionary in the field of economic, business and financial translation is the *Dictionnaire de la comptabilité et de la gestion financière* by Louis Ménard and collaborators. This bilingual dictionary is an English-French dictionary of terms used in accounting and in financial management containing French definition and translations of English entries. Although the dictionary can be bought electronically and on paper through the publisher (CPA and/or Institut Canadien des comptables agrees), most of the records and entries from this dictionary have been included in Termium Plus (see the unique entry for contributed capital in Termium which comes directly from this dictionary, source indicated).

Finally, the last but not the least primary resource of Canadian origin that I chose to cite as an important contribution to better specialized translation tools and learning in economics, business, and finance is the original and unparalleled "encyclopedic" bilingual Analytical Dictionary of Retailing by Jeanne Dancette and Christophe Réthoré published in 2000. This bilingual dictionary is a little gem in the subfield of marketing and commercial translation. This is due to the very large and encyclopedic nature of its content which brings tremendous specialized information and knowledge to help translators to understand and better translate specialized concepts and their interrelated concepts, their conceptual links with the entries being fully described.

Some secondary resources in financial translation from Canadian authors

Two typical Canadian secondary resources often cited are the two terminological databanks from Québec origin which are Termium Plus from le Bureau de la traduction of the Canadian Government, which was created at Université de Montréal in 1970 (Gagnon, 1994), and Le grand dictionnaire terminologique (GDT) from Office de la langue française du Québec of the Québec Government. With their free access and with the addition of some Spanish and Portuguese records in Termium Plus, these tools have gained an international userbase. One important distinction that can be made from a user's point of view is that Termium offers more translation-based equivalents while le GDT offers more rigorous terminological definitions in French (and in English) and is less interested in their interlinguistic translation or equivalent. By definition, these terminological databanks being general oriented offer specialized information on other fields of specialization than finance.

Another important secondary resources of Canadian origin is the Circuit magazine which is fully available on-line. One can find its most recent issue on-line as well as the full set of previous publications in an electronic format (https://www.circuitmagazine.org/archives). This reference material is not exclusively specialized in Finance but the magazine has published several issues on finance specialization or even on the economics of translation (issues number 126 (productivity and working conditions), 124 (project managers), 118 (translation market), 94 (advertising terms), 86 (translation management), 81 (insurance), 67 (translation industry), 66 (globalization), 65, 62 (streamlining), 37 (free trade), 35 (linguistic services management), 30 (business translation), 24 (translation industry), 21 (subcontracting), 20 (marketing), 14 (advertising)). There is also another publication centered on language wordings and phrases that is now searchable on-line. There is also a search engine provided with this publication which is called Chroniques de langue that can be used at this address: https://www.noslangues-ourlanguages.gc.ca/fr/chroniques-de-langue/index-fra. These last two publications are mostly written in French and generally address English to French translation problems. A similar secondary resource that focuses on English writing issues with several topics that relate to finance and business translation are the columns of the defunct publication Language Update which are still available on-line on the Favourite Article page here (https://www.noslangues-ourlanguages.gc.ca/fr/favourite-articles/index-fra).

As regards the very important volume of translation in relation with financial statements, there is a crucial secondary resource from CPA (chartered professional accountants) Canada that is dedicated to a better understanding of financial statements and which is published on-line in English and in French (in parallel). This publication/ web site is called "Reading financial statements: What do I need to know? FAQ." As is the case with most multilingual and bilingual on- line web pages, there is a language shortcut that allows the users to go to the same page in the other or in another language at the top of the page. Along with very detailed explanations on the function and usefulness of all pieces of financial statements, this document provides a full set of financial statements specimens in English and in French which contain de facto general English and French translation of most specialized terms used in financial statements documents or notes. Other than its usefulness as a primary resource, this reference material offer answers to many general and specific questions translators and readers might have regarding the information contained in these documents. Some readers may have a general idea of these answers by consulting the full page of questions that are answered through this resource.

As a fourth secondary resource, I must give a special mention to the Bulletin de terminologie on two volumes which was published mostly during the 80s and the 90s, before the advent of Internet and on-line access of specialized resources (a pdf format of most of the columns and bulletins was also published in the 2000s through the Ordre des comptables agréés du Québec). It's contribution is so important to the development and training of translators specialized in finance and economics that it's worth citing it here even though this publication is unfortunately not available anymore. We hope that this publication could be made available in the Internet as some of its material is still very relevant for language practitioners and translation learners. This was a periodical publication on terminological problems and their solutions in accounting and in finance. This publication was the fruit of the work of joint terminological efforts by accountants and translators. As a good example of its relevancy, there was a bulletin published in September 1995 (vol. 2, bulletin number 42-1) that was dedicated to the translation of corporate in French that is still useful for trainers in translation teaching classes today. An extract of the first page is provided below.

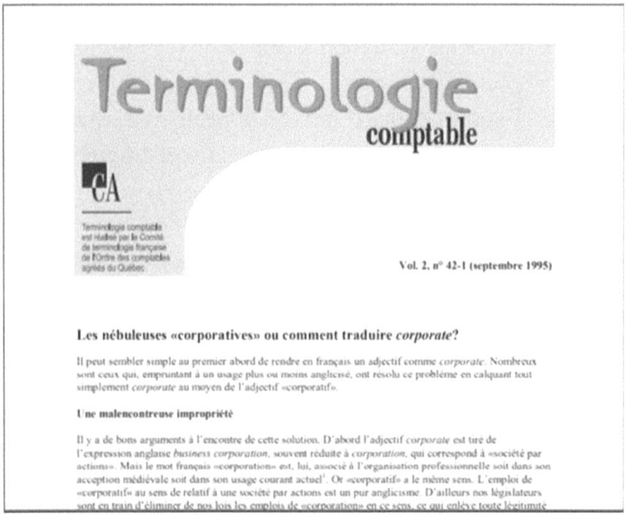

Terminologie comptable

CA

Terminologie comptable est réalisé par le Comité de terminologie française de l'Ordre des comptables agréés du Québec

Vol. 2, n° 42-1 (septembre 1995)

Les nébuleuses «corporatives» ou comment traduire *corporate*?

Il peut sembler simple au premier abord de rendre en français un adjectif comme *corporate*. Nombreux sont ceux qui, empruntant à un usage plus ou moins anglicisé, ont résolu ce problème en calquant tout simplement *corporate* au moyen de l'adjectif «corporatif».

Une malencontreuse impropriété

Il y a de bons arguments à l'encontre de cette solution. D'abord l'adjectif *corporate* est tiré de l'expression anglaise *business corporation*, souvent réduite à *corporation*, qui correspond à «société par actions». Mais le mot français «corporation» est, lui, associé à l'organisation professionnelle soit dans son acception médiévale soit dans son usage courant actuel[1]. Or «corporatif» a le même sens. L'emploi de «corporatif» au sens de relatif à une société par actions est un pur anglicisme. D'ailleurs nos législateurs sont en train d'éliminer de nos lois les emplois de «corporation» en ce sens, ce qui enlève toute légitimité

Figure 1. Terminologie comptable

In this bulletin, one can learn that corporate has two general meanings: one that means "relating to a business corporation or joint stock company." And another synecdoche using a part to refer to the whole that has three distinct uses: general or central services (as opposed to specialized or more technical departments or services), head office as opposed to branches and other installations, parent company, as opposed to subsidiaries. These explanations on the meaning in English are very enlightening in translation by making the translators aware of their exact referent which is not given or is difficult to seize or to remember, even in context, especially for beginners and/or second-language speakers.

Some tertiary resources in financial translation from Canadian authors

A first tertiary resource for financial translation in Canada is the Canadian Securities Administrators (CSA) web page that is joint efforts of the 10 provinces and 3 territories securities regulation organization in Canada. This resource offer investors different tools and resources to help them better manage their investment in the Canadian market. For education purposes, there is a section that provides access to securities rules and policies across Canada. A similar resource is available for each provinces and territories in Canada. In Québec, there is the web site of the Autorité des marchés financiers which offers a lot of information of financial nature, some of which is intended for professionals: insurers, brokers, firms, representatives and independent agents, deposit institutions and trust companies, securities and derivatives, market structures, and regulations and enforcement and some of which is intended for the general public: Insurance, Investments, Personal finances, Fraud prevention, Calculators and tools, Assistance and Complaints, Compensation and Deposit protection. These resources are very helpful to get an overview of existing documentation available in financial and economic translation and the first step to find detailed information on (and a better understanding of) certain types of investment and protections that are referred to in some texts.

There are also less formal reference materials which are subsection of existing web pages and are therefore more difficult to reference and share. This is the case for this page which is a sub element of the Collection of Canadian Language Resources web page and which contain a list of glossaries and dictionaries of finance and economics. https:// www.noslangues-ourlanguages.gc.ca/en/ressources-resources/index-eng Most of the time the documentation is provided for different fields of specialization including finance and economics. The fact that this is a subsection of a web page makes it more difficult to share and index these documents by fields of specialization.

Finally, for development purposes, a more traditional support is available through specialized classes in finance and economics, be it on-line or in presence. Some of these classes might even be free, such is the case with a massive open on-line course (MOOC) in personal finance designed and published by professors Boivin and Bachand (2015–2023) specialized in accounting at Université du Québec à Trois-Rivières. Chances are that all translation teachers might find of interest the publication of some of their colleagues who specialize in finance or economics. Most of the time these materials are intended for specialists but some of them might target general public, such as the MOOC from my colleagues.

In Canada, about 12 universities[1] are offering at least one course in specialized translation in either English to French exclusively or from French to English as well as from English to French (in both directions): Specialized translation courses are addressing finance and economics among other fields of specialization (administrative, legal, technical and scientific). Material and learning activities for these courses are less specialized and do not formally (with exceptions) present financial and business knowledge for translators. Most of the translation programs available in French offer one or two translation courses specialized in finance and economics (from English to French). Often, as it is the case at Université de Montréal, Université Laval and Concordia, one course is in economics and another one is in business (traduction commerciale), on the basis of the distinction between public and private activities of economic nature.

Some electronic material and documents of one of these courses is available for the public. This is partly the case for the course of economic and business translation introduction at Université de Montréal from Professor Chantal Gagnon at the Wiki page called Tradéco. Unfortunately, the matea rial and documents that are available to the public are of non-specialized nature and specialized ones in finance and economics are described among the other general ones.

1 Concordia University, McGill University, Ottawa University, Université Laval, Université de Moncton, Université de Montréal, Université du Québec en Outaouais, Université du Québec à Trois-Rivières, Université de Saint-Boniface, Université de Sherbrooke, York University and Toronto Metropolitan University.

Scientific and formal training resources in finance and economics translation

Another group of tertiary resources for translators are represented by scientific publications and textbooks in learning this field of specialization in translation.

From a Canadian perspective, there is firstly the seminal paper published by Jean Delisle in 1988 about what could be the ideal finance and economic translation course. What is interesting is that the ICEBFIT conference series can be considered as a response to a gap identified at the beginning of this paper for grouping together teachers and translators working in the business and economic field of specialization and addressing specific problems and topics relevant to this area of expertise and practice. The paper is innovative since it suggests learning objectives for this area of specialization and provides examples of learning activities in relation to these objectives. The author applies to the business and economic field of specialization its objective-based learning method that he deployed for general translation in its well-known manual.

Another more recent paper in this area of specialization is the one published by Marie-France Guénette (2022) on economic and commercial translation. The paper gives a general presentation of the area of specialization, with a tentative definition of the difference between financial translation encompassing macroeconomics and finance and commercial translation focusing more on business organization and activities (production, commercialization, human resources, management, finances, etc.). The separation of both areas can be connected with the more abstract separation we made between public activities of economic nature and private activities of economic nature. In the case of financial translation, Guénette (2022) suggests four sub-areas relevant to the translation practice: macroeconomics and regulation, accounting, banking and investment and insurance. Taking into account the importance of microeconomic concepts, I would suggest adding another topic of interest such as microeconomics and the circular economy model. In this module, the teacher could address supply and demand terminology and laws, among other key concepts.

There is also in Canada a collection of books from the ex-publishing house Linguatech created in 1975 by terminologist Robert Dubuc and now part of the Presses de l'Université de Montréal (PUM) since 2021 as the Linguatech collection. This small editor published some very important books in translation and in terminology from Québec authors, teachers and translators. Among the 50 books that were transferred to PUM, less than 10 address a topic (marketing, stock market, accounting, advertising) from the economic and financial area of specialization. The area of scientific and technical translation (with localization) seems to be better represented than economic and financial translation. Still, those books are another way for translators to develop their proficiency in their area of specialization.

Thirdly, there are also the different books and publications from Canadian authors that have contributed to the collections of papers published after the ICEBFIT Conferences in 2014, 2016, 2018 and 2021. There is a list of these books on the ICEBFIT previous Conference web pages https://dti.ua.es/en/tradeco/icebfit/2023/previous-conferences.html. Those publications are very important to the advances of knowledge in our area of specialization. They contain important discussions on the various links between theoretical parameters and practical requirements for the specialized translation to take place.

Fourthly, there is also a Canadian textbook entirely dedicated to learning the translation of economic and financial texts that has been published most recently in 2022. The author is Pier-Pascale Boulanger from Concordia University and her textbook is among the rare if not one of the first manual in Canada and in the world that is specialized in economy and in finance in the English-French direction of translation. This book is interesting for the very rich and interesting types of learning activities based on textual and notional operations. For example, one exercise is focusing on how to express the percentage difference of two percentage measures, and another one is on how to express changes in the economy in French (and avoid elliptical comparatives).

Part II: Information and datasets of Canadian origin for advances in economy and finance translation

The second and final part of this article looks to the future. It offers information that will be useful primarily for the advancement of knowledge in the field of specialization. It can also be said that this information will be useful for the further development of experienced specialist translators who already know the field fairly well, but who wish to deepen their knowledge of linguistic usage in the target language and of the denominations associated with key concepts in their field of specialization. At the same time, the information we provide in this section will also be useful to teachers responsible for these courses in professional translation training programs. It will help them to design and offer learners new training and learning materials (exercises). These types of resources are in a way multi-purpose, since they are raw data that can be used as primary, secondary or tertiary resources, depending on the situation.

The TERMIUM Plus terminology datasets provide useful information for the advancement of knowledge in economic and financial translation. These provide access to the full content of the terminology records in the large terminology database[2]. The datasets are provided according to the twenty or so major subdomains defined by the organization, almost half of which relate directly to economics and finance: administration, agriculture, construction, economics, home economics and hospitality, metallurgy, mining, petroleum, telecommunications and transport. The full content (definitions and contexts) of TERMIUM Plus records can be downloaded for research into the names and definitions of key concepts in our field of specialization. This data can also be used for the pedagogical design of specialized translation courses covering the key concepts of a field or several subfields (industries, transport, etc.). The datasets are published by Open Government, a project led by the Government of Canada, which is committed to transparency in its relations with its citizens.

Another resource which is instrumental in the design of specialized courses in financial and economic translation is the Canadian equivalent of the SEC's EDGAR, the U.S. electronic system for filing securities information. The Canadian site is called SEDAR. This service "provides access to most public securities documents and information filed by issuers with the thirteen provincial and territorial securities regulatory authorities ('Canadian Securities Administrators' or 'CSA') in the SEDAR filing

2 According to the Web site, the data maintenance and update are annual. At the time of going into press, the most recent modifications are dated February, 6, 2023.

system." The documents that are accessible through those services include all quarterly and annual financial statements and detailed annual information form as well as press releases on changes in senior management and other events having financial implications.

As opposed to documents provided by EDGAR which are monolingual English, what is very interesting regarding the Canadian SEDAR is that the documents filled for investors must be for a large part (for the provincial and territorial securities regulatory authorities which requires it) in English and in French. This mandatory requirement for most of the Canadian companies makes it possible to create a parallel corpora of financial statements and of other accounting documents and press releases and annual reports from registered companies and use these parallel corpora for different activities such as specialized translation, teaching and research (textual data or terminographic data).

A third Canadian data resource that I often use for research and teaching purposes in business, economic and financial translation is the Tradooit bilingual concordancer which is freely available on-line (see the reference section). What is truly unique about this bilingual concordancer and very original compared with other similar tools is the special index provided with each research result in the parallel corpora, which lists all the various target language equivalent expressions of the source language research key with their respective number of occurrences. This feature is very useful to grasp the extend of all translation solutions and to get a quick view of the most common and recurrent ones, compared to the more creative and original ones.

A fourth Canadian data resource that is useful for specialized translation in finance and in business are the sites of the thesaurus of government activities which provides a list of key terms to use when searching for information in the government web sites. These sites are useful for all the terminology related to public institutions and public activities such as social policies and administrative names and designations. In Canada, there are a federal and provincial web sites that one can consult in English and in French. On the federal level, there is the bilingual Government of Canada Core Subject Thesaurus, for which one can download the dataset (4,991 terms in English and 5,059 in French, including 2,299 preferred terms in English and 2,300 in French). There are also other datasets that might be useful in this area and that are published by the government of Canada.

On the provincial levels, there are the Government terms for the government of Ontario (bilingual reference material) and the Thésaurus de l'activité gouvernementale from the government of Québec. These resources contain terminological data and selected or "official" terms (and their standard or "official" translation) that can be used directly in target-text or bilingual revision or that can be processed and compared for the purpose of translating documents related to government activities such as public debates, health and national security, and finance and economy. From a cultural point of view, these hierarchies of terms may be used to compare denominations of specific concepts in a specific language culture. They might also be useful regarding collocations and most frequent terms used in relation to government activities. As opposed to the previous textual data that can be found on private sector activities, these resources are very handy for establishing standard or preferred terminology in public or governmental activities.

Finally, a last resource is the provincial and federal budget web pages (archived or most recent ones) that contain a lot of texts that can be aligned for research and translation purposes. Each provincial, territorial and federal government in Canada provide once a year a detailed budget plan in which the elected members of the government announce what their financial projects will be to protect the economic health of the country or the province and territory. In the budget plan, each government also makes available the state of the public finances and of the public debt or surplus (in the rare case when this happens). The budget plan is usually described in different documents containing often 500 to 1000 pages altogether with one summary document of only 30 to 50 pages.

These documents are evidently very useful for translators as a primary resource when they are provided in two or more languages. As a unilingual documentation, these documents can also be handy for target language specialized terminology and for teaching and learning public finance key concepts and knowledge. In Canada, official and non-official bilingual governments publish their yearly budget plan in the two official languages such as English and French (federal government, Ontario, Québec, New Brunswick, Manitoba, Yukon and Nunavut). Some of this documentation by the government in Ontario, such as the press release announcing the new budget plan, is made available in 20 languages, including English and French. See for example the 2023 Ontario budget web page at https://budget.ontario.ca/2023/index.html.

Accompanying the budget plan documentation, there are also analytical documents of the budget plans prepared and published by the major accounting firms in the country (which are the same as the big four accounting firms (and professional service networks) in the world, such as Deloitte, Ernst & Young (EY), KPMG, and PwC).

In this second part of the paper, I have shown some resources that may contribute to empirical studies in translation based on textual data (from parallel corpora in corpus-based translation studies) and on terminographic data from terminology databanks (terminography studies which is the use of terminology data for translation or cultural purposes).

I hope that the data provided in this last part of the paper will help translators and other researchers in translation to get a better knowledge of two different and complementary segments of translation and terminology users who are, the individual private activities and the collective public activities.

Conclusion

In this paper, I have provided a very large overview of Canadian specialized resources, datasets and information that might be useful for learning, teaching and studying specialized translation in economy and finance. I hope that these resources I've provided here will be useful to other practitioners and teachers in economic and financial translation. I have used myself these resources in the preparation of studies on subjects in the field of economic and financial translation, as well as in the preparation of material for the courses I've been giving in economic and financial translation over the past few years.

I would like to insist on the importance of research in financial and economic translation for the creation of better learning materials and professional training courses. In specialized translation, research is crucial in the virtuous circle of scientific knowledge: more research contribute to a better knowledge of translation skills required for specialized translation which in turn makes it possible to improve the content of training courses in specialized translation.

Economic and financial translation in Canada is supported by a range of primary, secondary, and tertiary resources. Corpus studies will inevitably play a crucial role in enhancing the teaching and learning of financial translation, offering empirical insights and improving translation practices. As technology continues to advance, it is essential to find and describe how the human expertise will need to be deployed in complement with new machine translation based on AI features. Professionals in the field of economic and financial translation, both in Canada and worldwide, will be able to effectively address the demands of our increasingly globalized economy and technologically-driven translation practices by seamlessly integrating technological advantages with their robust theoretical knowledge and practical skills, fortified and grounded in empirical research and studies.

Acknowledgements

This piece of research was performed as part of the project "Business translation and research. A bibliometric stuy" (PID2020-112930GB-I00). This is a Research + Development + Innovation project which is part of the Spanish programmes designed to generate and consolidate scientific and technological knowledge with a social leaning in its 2020 edition by the Spanish Ministry of Science and Innovation.

References

Autorité des marchés financiers (2023), L'Autorité des marchés financiers, https://lautorite.qc.ca/en/general-public, last accessed on September 29, 2023.

Boivin, M. & Bachand, M. (2015–2023). *La littératie financière et fiscale ouverte à tous*, last accessed on September 29, 2023. https://oraprdnt.uqtr.uquebec.ca/pls/public/gscw031?owa_no_site=1318&owa_no_fiche=7

Boulanger, P. (2022). *Apprendre à traduire les textes économiques de l'anglais au français*. Montréal: Éditions JFD.

Cohen, B. (2023). *Lexique de cooccurrents* (2e édition revue et augmentée). Montréal: Presses de l'Université de Montréal.

CSA / ACVM (2023), Canadian Securities Administrators, https://www.securities-administrators.ca/, last accessed on September 29, 2023.

Dancette, J. & Réthoré, C. (2000). *Dictionnaire analytique de la distribution = Analytical Dictionary of Retailing*. Montréal: Presses de l'Université de Montréal.

Delisle, J. (1988). L'initiation à la traduction économique. *Meta,* 33(2): 204–215.

Gagnon, C. (2021). *Tradéco – Introduction à la traduction économique et commerciale, Ressources électroniques section*, last accessed on July 2, 2023. http://tradeco.pbworks.com/w/page/47026137/Accueil.

Gagnon, R. (1994). Les grandes banques de terminologie. *Meta,* 39(3): 498–520.

Gallego- Hernandez, D. (2014). Presentación: hacia une triangulación entre docencia, investigación y profesión en el marco de la traducción económica. In D. Gallego-Hernandez (Ed.), *Traducción económica: entre profesión, formación y recursos documentales.* Vertere: Monográficos de la Revista Hermeneus, no. 16.

Government of Canada Core Subject Thesaurus, Library and Archives Canada, last accessed on September 29, 2023. https://open.canada.ca/data/en/dataset/d4a0e406-eea9-41a7-bcae-28c31f3b9c65

Government terms (Ontario), Government of Ontario, last accessed on September 29, 2023. https://open.canada.ca/data/en/dataset/da69f96f-4075-477e-9ab2-c1bec97faa75

Guénette, Marie-France. (2022). Economic and financial translation: key factors for successful training. *Translation Matters,* 4(2), special issue on Translation and Money.

Mel'čuk, I. (1996). Wanner, Leo (Ed.). Lexical functions: A tool for the description of lexical relations in a lexicon. *Lexical Functions in Lexicography and Natural Language Processing,* 37: 102.

Ménard, L. et al. (2011–2021). *Dictionnaire de la comptabilité et de la gestion financière : anglais- français avec index français- anglais* (3rd ed.). Institut canadien des comptables agréés, version 3.2 on line, last accessed on September 29, 2023. https://www.cpacanada.ca/fr/ressources-en-comptabilite-et-en-affaires/domaines-connexes/technologies-et-gestion-de-linformation/publications/dictionnaire

Ménard, L. & Dandonneau, A. (2009). *Dictionary of derivatives and other financial instruments*. Ordre des comptables professionnels agréés du Québec, last accessed on September 29, 2023. https://dictionnaire.cpaquebec.ca/.

Poirier, É. (2010). Quand la technologie se met au service d'une véritable bidirectionnalité… *Circuit*, 106: 26.

Poirier, É. (2012). Entre dictionnaire et lexique, entre œuvre pionnière et classique, *Circuit*, 117: 24.

SEDAR, Canadian Securities Administrators, last accessed on September 29, 2023. www.sedar.com.

TERMIUM Plus®, the Government of Canada's terminology and linguistic data bank (September, 25, 2016), Public Services and Procurement Canada, https://open.canada.ca/data/en/dataset/94fc74d6-9b9a-4c2e-9c6c-45a5092453aa, last accessed on September 29, 2023.

TradooIT Bilingual Concordancer, last accessed on September 29 2023. https://www.tradooit.com.

Thésaurus de l'activité gouvernementale, gouvernement du Québec, last accessed on September 29, 2023. https://www.thesaurus.gouv.qc.ca/tag/accueil.do;jsessionid=542E36BA2798BF87CB3F8ACEAD0C3117

Danio Maldussi

7 « The Lady is not tapering » ou l'euphémisme en tant que figure de la médiation, entre euphémismes métonymiques et tabous

The art of argumentation among central bank governors, often referred to as « oracles of money » (Orioli, 2016), involves a delicate balance of conveying messages while withholding information. This article examines one of the more recent Anglicisms to permeate institutional communication: *tapering*, a term used to describe the gradual reduction of securities purchases under the *PEPP* (Pandemic Emergency Purchase Programme). Coined by Ben Bernanke, the former chairman of the US Federal Reserve, *tapering* serves, at least in its initial intentions, as a euphemistic strategy to soften the blow of an abrupt halt to securities purchases. Interestingly, *tapering* is not only a tool of central banks, but is also used by critics of the European Central Bank (*ECB*) who advocate an end to asset purchases. For these critics, *tapering* becomes a rhetorical weapon used to challenge the *ECB*'s policy of recalibrating purchases rather than reducing them outright. As a result, *tapering* has become a source of anxiety and even perceived as a threat within the financial community. This has led Christine Lagarde, the President of the *ECB*, to adopt a defensive stance, countering the *tapering* discourse with the metonymic euphemism of *recalibration*. This response is strategically aimed at diverting attention from the potentially negative implications of *tapering*. In sum, this metonymic euphemism serves not only as a means of softening the impact, but also as a mediation tool within the broader context of the *ECB*'s communication strategy, known as *forward guidance*, a practice originally initiated by Mario Draghi.

Introduction

Dans un article qui s'intitule « Aspects perlocutoires, discursifs et traductionnels dans la terminologie des banques centrales : de la politique de 'forward guidance' au programme de 'quantitative easing' » (Maldussi, 2019) nous nous sommes attardés sur le comportement en discours de ces deux termes qui constituent le trait distinctif du mandat de Mario Draghi à la Présidence de la Banque centrale européenne (dorénavant *BCE*). Aux fins de cette nouvelle contribution, il est utile de rappeler en préambule que *Quantitative Easing* (dorénavant *QE*) est, selon la définition qu'en donne la Banque de France (2021) :

> un outil de politique monétaire non conventionnelle. Utilisé pour lutter contre le risque de déflation et de récession, il consiste, pour une banque centrale, à intervenir de façon massive, généralisée et prolongée sur les marchés financiers en achetant des actifs (notamment des titres de dette publique) aux banques commerciales et à d'autres acteurs. Ces achats massifs entraînent une baisse des taux d'intérêt. Cela permet aux ménages, aux entreprises et aux États de continuer à se financer à de bonnes conditions, favorisant la croissance économique et la remontée du taux d'inflation à un niveau compatible avec la stabilité des prix.

Sujet des plus controversés et critiqués, le *QE* est un outil à l'égard duquel Mario Draghi a adopté celle que nous qualifions de véritable stratégie de l'évitement, esquivant soigneusement de reprendre le terme *QE* dans ses réponses aux journalistes dans le but de ne pas être assimilé à la politique de la *FED* (Federal Reserve américaine, dorénavant *FED*), qui utilisa amplement le *QE* et qui, au vu de ses statuts, a des objectifs politiques et économiques tout à fait différents.

Dans un autre article qui s'intitule « Guerre des isotopies dans la conceptualisation de la néologie d'emprunt: le « quantitative easing » de la *BCE* et sa figuralité à l'épreuve du discours de presse francophone » (Maldussi, 2020) nous avons approfondi le rôle des isotopies, des métaphores et des métonymies en tant que catalyseurs d'écoles de pensée fédératrices opposées, reflet de différentes visions de l'Europe.

Ces deux premières contributions ont constitué les prémisses afin d'étayer notre nouvelle réflexion sur des bases plus solides. Le déclic de la présente recherche a été l'apparition dans la Communication de la *BCE* de l'emprunt intégral *tapering* qui visiblement, au fil des mois, est devenu le trait distinctif qui condense les polémiques autour de la ligne politique du mandat de Christine Lagarde à la tête de la *BCE*. *Tapering*, utilisé pour la première fois dans l'histoire par Ben Bernanke, ancien Gouverneur de la *FED* du 1er février 2006 au 31 janvier 2014, indique une réduction graduelle des achats de titres de la part de la Banque centrale américaine. Une réduction, comme nous aurons l'occasion de l'analyser, qui a été au contraire perçue comme la fin du *QE* et donc la fin des aides à l'économie, transformant le terme en un tabou.

Qu'est-ce que *QE* et *tapering* ont en commun? Assez curieusement, les deux termes font partie de la longue controverse et des polémiques qui enflamment les débats européens sur les mesures de lutte contre la crise et sont tous deux utilisés comme des accusations. Dans le premier cas, l'accusation portée contre Mario Draghi est celle de mettre en œuvre une politique soi-disant américaine; dans le second, l'insinuation formulée contre Christine Lagarde par les partisans d'une politique accommodante est que la Présidente de la BCE arrête le rythme des achats dans le cadre du *PEPP* (Pandemic Emergency Purchase Programme), avec pour conséquence de laisser l'économie livrée à elle-même. *QE* et *tapering*, au vu de leur caractère polémique, s'apparenteraient, à quelques différences près, à ceux que Gallie (1956) appelait des « essentially contested concepts », se référant en particulier au domaine de la politique, à savoir des concepts autour desquels se déchaînent les polémiques les plus âpres et les interprétations les plus disparates, à tel point de rendre impossible l'élaboration d'une position unifiante, comme dans le cas des concepts de démocratie et de liberté. Si d'un côté ces deux dernières notions sont amplement partagées dans l'absolu, de l'autre côté beaucoup de divergences restent pour ce qui est de leur implémentation. Comme c'est bien le cas pour *QE* et *tapering*.

Revenons au focus de notre recherche. Les deux termes, *QE* et *tapering*, sont unis par le fait qu'ils n'apparaissent que dans la session des Questions/Réponses et donc non pas dans le texte des Conférences de presse. *Tapering*, au vu de la réaction de Christine Lagarde, s'avère être un terme fortement anxiogène, voire menaçant auprès de l'univers financier. Sa simple évocation de la part des journalistes donne lieu, en réaction, à des énonciations à forte valeur euphémistique.

Dans le cas du *QE*, c'est bien la figuralité qui entoure son utilisation dans la presse (l'emploi de la métonymie de la « planche à billets », de la part de ses détracteurs, est éclairante à cet égard) à faire entrevoir l'existence de camps de pensée opposés. Qu'en est-il de *tapering*? Dans ce cas, comme nous l'avons fait pour *QE*, il s'avère intéressant d'analyser l'antidote utilisé par Christine Lagarde visant à contrecarrer les effets nocifs induits par le *tapering* en tant que tabou brandi sciemment, notamment l'euphémisme métonymique du *recalibrage*. Ce dernier est l'équivalent de traduction de « recalibration » repéré dans notre sous-corpus qui réunit les Conférences de presse de Christine Lagarde en langue française.

Dans un premier temps, après avoir présenté les fondements théoriques et méthodologiques ainsi que le choix de nos sous-corpus, nous esquisserons brièvement le rôle des Gouverneurs des Banques centrales et l'adoption, tout d'abord de la part de Mario Draghi et ensuite de Christine Lagarde, de la politique des annonces dite de *Forward Guidance*, une stratégie qui prévoit la communication d'indications prospectives au bénéfice des acteurs des marchés financiers. Dans un deuxième temps, après une brève analyse de l'origine du *tapering*, nous étudierons le fonctionnement de cette énonciation euphémique et ses rapports avec la métonymie, avec quelques références à un autre terme à valeur euphémique, qui s'insère dans le débat politique toujours en réaction à l'épouvantail de la baisse des achats de titres et qui partage avec *tapering* le sème de la baisse progressive: *tilting*. En particulier, nous soulignerons le rôle de l'euphémisme métonymique du *recalibrage*, lequel de simple figure de l'atténuation, se transforme en véritable figure de la médiation entre les objectifs de la communication institutionnelle de la BCE et les acteurs des marchés financiers, le tout dans le cadre et au service de la politique des annonces.

Fondements théoriques et fondements méthodologiques

Sur le plan théorique, en matière d'étude des procédés néologiques euphémiques, notre point de départ est l'analyse de Sablayrolles (2016). Pour ce qui est des relations liant le tabou et l'euphémisme et du caractère des euphémismes néosémiques, nos essais de référence sont, respectivement, López Díaz (2018) et López Díaz (2016). À propos des effets de type euphémisants et de la polyphonie divergente en tant que positionnement critique à l'égard des euphémismes, nous nous inspirons respectivement des réflexions de Bonhomme (2012) et de Bonhomme (2020). En ce qui concerne l'euphémisme en tant que stratégie d'atténuation nous

nous inspirons de Jaubert (2008). Pour ce qui est de l'étude de la reformulation en tant que moyen linguistique pour démasquer les euphémismes, notre essai de référence est Kacprzak (2022). En ce qui concerne l'interprétation métonymique ainsi que les effets illocutoires de la métonymie, notre ouvrage de référence est Bonhomme (2006). Pour ce qui est de la figuralité non pas en tant que simple ornement mais en tant que figuralité conceptuelle de l'interaction communicative, notre ouvrage de référence est Prandi (2021).

Choix des sous-corpus et aspects méthodologiques

Les observations et les conclusions de notre recherche se feront à partir de quatre sous-corpus. Les trois premiers sous-corpus sont tirés du site de la *BCE*. Ces derniers regroupent les conférences de presse de Christine Lagarde en langue anglaise, française et italienne depuis qu'elle a pris ses fonctions le 1er novembre 2019 à la tête de la *BCE*, notamment à partir de la conférence du 12 décembre 2019 jusqu'à celle du 27 juillet 2023. En ce qui concerne le contenu des différentes versions linguistiques, la version anglaise fait autorité[1]. Les conférences sont accompagnées par les sessions de Questions/Réponses, ces dernières n'étant disponibles qu'en langue anglaise[2]. Le quatrième sous-corpus regroupe les articles de presse française en ligne contenant les termes *tapering* et *recalibrage*, recueillis grâce au logiciel *BootCat*[3]. L'objectif de ce dernier sous-corpus est celui de repérer la cohorte métalinguistique qui entoure les deux termes[4]. Après

1 La formulation précise à la fin de chaque conférence est la suivante: « Veuillez consulter la version anglaise pour les termes exacts approuvés par le Conseil des gouverneurs ».

2 Les Conférences de presse de Christine Lagarde, ainsi que les séances de Questions-Réponses, sont disponibles sur le site de la *BCE*.

3 *BootCat* est disponible à l'adresse suivante: https://bootcat.dipintra.it/?section=home.

4 Le nombre total des mots est de 125.789. Ce sous-corpus réunit les articles tirés de sites de presse spécialisée tels que, entre autres, *investir.lesechos.fr*, *optionfinance.fr*, *morningstar.fr*, *latribune.fr*, *alternatives-economiques.fr*, *capital.fr*, etc. Nous tenons à préciser qu'au vu de la relative exiguïté de ce sous-corpus, nous nous réservons de valider les résultats de notre recherche à partir d'un sous-corpus plus ample.

avoir été convertis en codage *UTF-8*, les sous-corpus ont été explorés à l'aide du logiciel de gestion des données *Sketch Engine*[5]. La recherche que nous menons ici grâce à une approche de type ascendant s'insère dans un cadre sémantico-pragmatique : c'est bien grâce à l'entourage verbal des expressions nouvelles sur lesquelles nous allons nous focaliser que nous pourrons mettre en exergue leur caractère tabouisant ou euphémisant.

La politique des annonces ou l'art de bien communiquer

L'utilisation d'un langage feutré voire habilement et délibérément obscur de la part des Gouverneurs des banques centrales afin d'éviter la surchauffe des marchés financiers est bien connue. Célèbre est à ce propos le jargon impénétrable dénommé *Green Speak* inventé par Alan Greenspan, ancien président de la FED[6]. Du reste, la rhétorique est l'art de l'argumentation et chaque Gouverneur (du latin *gubernator*, timonnier) est connu pour son style. C'est l'art de « dire » et de « ne pas dire », le « dit » et le « non-dit »: les Gouverneurs tissent un rapport controversé entre explicite ou sens de l'énoncé et implicite en tant que sous-entendu. De véritables « Oracles de la monnaie » pour reprendre le titre du volume d'Orioli (2016) consacré à l'art de la parole dans le langage des banquiers centraux. Ou, tout au moins, jusqu'au mandat de Mario Draghi qui inaugure en 2013 la politique des annonces, une stratégie qui se fonde sur la communication systématique de données prospectives. Objectif : gérer les attentes des acteurs des marchés financiers, expliquer la complexité, réduire l'incertitude, ce qui est aussi une question d'autorité perçue: que l'on songe à la célèbre réponse de Mario Draghi du 26 juillet 2012 face à la crise de l'euro : le *Whatever it*

5 *Sketchengine* est disponible à l'adresse suivante: https://www.sketchengine.eu/.
6 Exemplaire à ce propos l'anecdote suivante : « He used to take pride in the resulting obfuscation – even characterizing his own way of communicating as 'mumbling with great incoherence'. In a famous incident, he once told a US senator who claimed to have understood what the famously obscurantist chairman had just said, « in that case, 'I must have misspoken' » (Blinder, 2001: 66). [« Il était fier de l'obscurité qui en résultait, allant même jusqu'à qualifier sa propre façon de communiquer de 'marmonnement tout à fait incohérent'. Lors d'un incident célèbre, il a rèpondu à un sénateur américain qui prétendait avoir compris ce que le célèbre président obscurantiste venait de dire: 'Dans ce cas, j'ai dû mal m'exprimer'». Notre traduction].

takes est désormais un néologisme à part entière qui est recensé par l'Encyclopédie *Treccani* (2020). Une autorité bien perçue si la journaliste Longo, dans le quotidien financier italien *Il Sole 24 Ore*, titre son article sur la valeur de la crédibilité d'un Président du Conseil « Quanto vale l'effetto Draghi sullo spread? Un miliardo di risparmi potenziali » [« Combien vaut l'effet Draghi sur le spread? Un milliard d'économies potentielles ». Notre traduction] (Longo, 2021, en ligne).

La politique des annonces consiste en des « indications sur l'orientation future de la politique monétaire » de la part de la *BCE*, à savoir « des informations sur ses intentions concernant sa politique monétaire à venir, sur la base de son évaluation des perspectives de stabilité des prix » (BCE, 2017). La communication systématique de données prospectives « améliore donc l'efficacité de la politique monétaire de la *BCE* et aide celle-ci à réaliser son principal objectif: être au service des Européens en maintenant la stabilité des prix dans toute la zone euro » (BCE, 2017). Un exemple révélateur et concret est celui présenté sur le site de la *BCE* : la Banque centrale fait une annonce concernant sa politique monétaire, à savoir que les taux directeurs[7] devraient rester bas dans le futur, ce qui fait que les banques commerciales, à leur tour, sont plus susceptibles de baisser les taux sur les prêts à long terme. Conséquence : le loyer de l'argent pourra baisser au bénéfice des entreprises et des particuliers, stimulant ainsi l'investissement et les dépenses (BCE, 2017).

En particulier, cette stratégie se révèle efficace, voire nécessaire, quand la BCE veut réduire encore plus les taux d'intérêt qui sont déjà très bas :

> [d]ans de telles circonstances, une communication claire autour des intentions en matière de politique monétaire à venir aide les banques, les intervenants des marchés financiers, les entreprises et les consommateurs à mieux comprendre comment les coûts d'emprunt sont susceptibles d'évoluer à l'avenir, et donne à l'économie l'impulsion dont elle a besoin (BCE, 2017).

---

7 Pour la définition de taux directeurs, nous renvoyons à l'explication donnée par Wikipédia : « Les taux directeurs sont les taux d'intérêt au jour le jour fixés par la banque centrale d'un pays ou d'une union monétaire, et qui permettent à celle-ci de réguler l'activité économique ». https://fr.wikipedia.org/wiki/Taux_directeur.

Le terme *guidance* contient déjà une orientation future étant donné qu'il s'agit spécifiquement des prévisions de bilan qu'une entreprise communique aux marchés et qu'elle s'engage à respecter. L'ajout de *forward* amplifie son contenu de futurité. La confirmation de l'orientation future communiquée précédemment est à la source d'inférences prédictives positives de la part des investisseurs et se reflète favorablement sur les cours de Bourse. La politique des annonces constitue le cadre dans lequel s'insère l'euphémisme métonymique du *recalibrage* utilisé par Christine Lagarde visant à déjouer le tabou du *tapering*.

« The Lady is not tapering » : origine d'un emprunt intégral à valeur euphémisante

Désormais célèbre, à l'occasion de la Conférence de presse du 9 septembre 2021, est la réponse de Christine Lagarde à la question précise de la part de la presse lors de la session des Questions/Réponses : « Would you characterise this (the end of PEPP), or did you characterise this internally, as a taper, or is it a turning point, or how would you characterise the move? » [« Caractériseriez-vous cela (la fin du PEPP), ou l'avez-vous caractérisé en interne, comme une réduction graduelle, ou est-ce qu'il s'agit d'un tournant, ou comment caractériseriez-vous cette évolution? ». Notre traduction]. Christine Lagarde faisant écho à la célèbre réponse de l'ancien premier Ministre britannique Margaret Thatcher « The lady's not for turning »[8] réagit de la façon suivante :

> I would preface my response to your first question by a quote, actually, in a way, which is, the lady isn't tapering. Because what we are doing is recalibrating PEPP, which I'll remind you is the Pandemic Emergency Purchase Programme, and we are recalibrating just as we did back in December and back in March. [Je commencerai ma réponse à votre première question par une citation, en fait, d'une

---

8 « To those waiting with bated breath for that favourite media catchphrase, the 'U-turn', I have only one thing to say. 'You turn if you want to. The lady's not for turning.' I say that not only to you, but to our friends overseas – and also to those who are not our friends ». Traduction française (Golder, 2019 : 84): « À ceux qui retiennent leur souffle dans l'attente de ce slogan des médias, le 'revirement', je n'ai qu'une chose à dire. 'Opérez un demi-tour si vous le voulez. La dame n'est pas en faveur d'une volte-face'. Je ne le dis pas seulement à vous, mais aussi à nos amis d'outre-mer – ainsi qu'à ceux qui ne sont pas nos amis ».

certaine manière, à savoir que la dame n'est pas en train de réduire ses achats de titres. Car ce que nous faisons, c'est recalibrer le PEPP, qui, je vous le rappelle, est le programme d'achat d'urgence face à la pandémie, et nous le recalibrons comme nous l'avons fait au mois de décembre et de mars. Notre traduction].

L'assertion de Christine Lagarde selon laquelle elle ne serait pas en train de procéder à un *tapering* mais plutôt à un *recalibrage*, une réponse qui « n'a pas empêché de nombreux observateurs d'interpréter cette décision comme un 'tapering' qui ne dit pas son nom » (Option Finance, 2021), met encore une fois en lumière l'affrontement interne au sein de l'*Eurotower* sur la durée du *PEPP*, le programme d'achat d'obligations de 1850 milliards d'euros lancé au début du déploiement de la Covid-19 dans la zone euro (Affaritaliani.it., 2021), les faucons de l'Europe du Nord insistant pour la cessation complète des achats (Adviseonly, 2021). Une polémique qui rappelle celle qui a marqué le débat sur la politique d'expansion monétaire et à laquelle participent les mêmes actants: la *BCE* en tant que patient sur le banc des accusés et les pays de l'Europe du Nord en tant qu'agents. Le circonstant, lui aussi, reste le même : l'*Eurotower*, un emploi métonymique pour indiquer le siège de la *BCE*.

Le verbe *to taper*, selon la définition qu'en donne le *Cambridge Dictionary* en ligne, signifie « to become gradually narrower at one end, or to make something do this » « se rétrécir progressivement, ou faire en sorte que quelque chose le devienne ». Notre traduction]. *Tapering* est un nom de procès issu d'un verbe (de l'anglais *to taper*), à l'instar de *QE* (de l'anglais *to ease*).

Analysons tout d'abord l'origine de cet emprunt à la langue anglo-américaine. Comme nous l'avons déjà souligné dans notre Introduction, *tapering* est un terme créé par l'ancien Président de la *FED*, Ben Bernanke, pour éviter d'annoncer dramatiquement la fin du *QE* aux États-Unis. *Tapering* prend la forme d'une tentative de minimiser les effets d'un brusque arrêt des achats de titres de la part de la Banque centrale américaine, ce qui pourrait provoquer la surchauffe des marchés et une véritable panique auprès des investisseurs, avec des retombées au niveau international au vu de la mondialisation de la finance et des places boursières. Or, « [l]e 'tapering' est devenu une sorte d'obsession chez de nombreux commentateurs boursiers qui semblent tout simplement assimiler cette notion à celle de 'resserrement' » (Option Finance, 2021). À tel point que cette terreur a donné naissance à un autre néologisme d'emprunt : *tapertantrum*[9], littéralement une colère, une inquiétude à son paroxysme à la suite de la simple annonce du *taper*, qui, aux États-Unis, a causé une hausse des taux longs, faisant flamber les rendements des *T-bonds*, les bons du trésor américains. Comme l'écrit Jean-Paul Betbèze, Professeur émérite de l'université Panthéon Assas, qui dans le terme *taper* entrevoit aussi une référence religieuse étant donné que *taper* est aussi la petite chandelle à la disposition des fidèles à l'église pour allumer un cierge, ce qui lui permet de jouer sur la métaphore de la flamme :

> « To taper » : diminuer graduellement, effiler, rendre plus étroit. Ce verbe anglais vient du nom « taper », cierge. Une référence religieuse dans la finance, comme si ce tapering de la banque centrale, qui la ferait acheter graduellement moins de bons du Trésor pour financer le déficit budgétaire, allait éteindre la flamme de la reprise ! En tout cas, c'est la crainte des marchés et des banquiers centraux qui ne veulent pas voir... rallumée une inquiétude qui ferait trop remonter les taux longs aux Etats-Unis, puis partout ailleurs. [...]
>
> On pourra toujours dire que c'est confondre le ralentissement des achats de bons du Trésor avec le changement d'orientation de la politique monétaire, mais le mal était fait. Les marchés financiers ont traduit « relativement moins accommodant » en « plus restrictif », à l'extrême surprise de Bernanke. Depuis lors, le problème demeure : comment éviter que se reproduise ce revirement des marchés?

Tapering finit donc par se transformer en mot tabou, malgré les bonnes intentions de son créateur. Or, le *tapering* est défendu par les détracteurs de la *BCE*, favorables à la fin des achats de titres, et par conséquent brandi

9 Comme l'indique le site *Investopedia*, « [t]he phrase, taper tantrum, describes the 2013 surge in U.S. Treasury yields, resulting from the Federal Reserve's (Fed) announcement of future tapering of its policy of quantitative easing. The Fed announced that it would be reducing the pace of its purchases of Treasury bonds, to reduce the amount of money it was feeding into the economy. The ensuing rise in bond yields in reaction to the announcement was referred to as a taper tantrum in financial media » https://www.investopedia.com/terms/t/taper-tantrum.asp. [« L'expression 'taper tantrum' désigne la hausse des rendements des obligations du Trésor américain en 2013, à la suite de l'annonce par la Réserve fédérale (Fed) d'une réduction progressive de sa politique d'expansion monétaire. La Fed a annoncé qu'elle réduirait le rythme de ses achats d'obligations du Trésor, afin de diminuer la quantité d'argent qu'elle injectait dans l'économie. La hausse des rendements obligataires à la suite de cette annonce a été qualifiée de 'taper tantrum' par les médias financiers ». Notre traduction].

comme une arme contre la politique de la *BCE*. Ce qui oblige Christine Lagarde à se mettre sur la défensive : la Présidente de la *BCE* reformule le terme *tapering* dans ses réponses aux journalistes pour affirmer que, du point de vue sémantique, il n'appartient pas à sa politique ou du moins ce n'est pas exactement ce qu'elle fait quand elle modifie sa politique d'achat de titres. Au contraire, elle procède à un *recalibrage* des achats de titres. S'il est indéniable qu'avec le *tapering* nous nous trouvons face à un culturème issu d'une culture financière autre, il est tout aussi évident que l'aspect tabou n'est pas intrinsèque au terme. Plus précisément, il existe un effet manipulateur dans l'usage de ce terme qui fait qu'il soit brandi comme un tabou contre un adversaire bien précis.

Assez paradoxalement, la fin du *QE* par l'annonce du *tapering* devrait être considérée comme une bonne nouvelle étant donné que si un pays n'a plus besoin de soutiens de la part de sa Banque centrale, cela est un signe de bonne santé économique et financière et que la phase de redressement s'est achevée. Néanmoins, les craintes concernant en particulier la réaction des investisseurs et les éventuelles retombées sur les taux d'intérêt demeurent. Des retombées qui ne peuvent qu'entraîner la hausse de ces derniers, avec des conséquences négatives sur les emprunts de la part des entreprises et des ménages. Or, si l'on tient compte du fait que la réaction de la part des investisseurs est toujours « anticipée », il n'est pas étonnant qu'en cas d'absence de communication concernant le *tapering*, les investisseurs puissent penser que la *BCE* continue de nourrir des doutes sur la santé effective du pays concerné. La réaction anticipée du public des investisseurs et des décideurs politiques constitue à juste titre une activité inférentielle bien connue sur les marchés financiers et constitue un trait fondamental du fonctionnement de ces derniers[10].

Avant de nous focaliser sur la réponse de Christine Lagarde, nous mentionnons une autre expression euphémique qui fait son apparition le 14 juin 2021 lors du discours d'Isabel Schnabel – économiste allemande et membre du directoire de la Banque centrale européenne – et qui anticipe à juste titre le débat concernant la fin des achats de titres: *tilting*. Selon la définition qu'en donne le *Oxford Advanced Learner's Dictionary* (2023),

10 À ce propos nous renvoyons à Maldussi (2015).

to tilt signifie : « to move, or make something move, into a position with one side or end higher than the other » [« déplacer ou faire déplacer quelque chose dans une position où un côté ou une extrémité est plus élevé que l'autre ». Notre traduction]. Selon cette stratégie, la *BCE* devrait non pas baisser le rythme des achats mais plutôt réorienter ses achats vers des titres de sociétés écologiquement responsables :

> Another possibility would be to pursue a more sophisticated 'tilting strategy' under which the ECB could adjust its monetary policy operations more gradually in line with sustainability considerations [...]. Given the still nascent state of the green bond market, tilting towards this particular market may, however, adversely affect market liquidity or unduly influence the price discovery mechanism. Therefore, one could consider tilting strategies that also favour issuers that have a clear path and commitment to reducing their greenhouse gas emissions. Tilting strategies could be performed at the level of sectors, firms or bonds. (Schnabel 2021, en ligne). [Une autre possibilité serait de poursuivre une 'stratégie de migration' plus sophistiquée dans le cadre de laquelle la BCE pourrait ajuster ses opérations de politique monétaire plus graduellement en fonction de considérations de durabilité [...]. Étant donné l'état encore naissant du marché des obligations vertes, la migration vers ce marché particulier pourrait toutefois affecter négativement la liquidité du marché ou influencer indûment le mécanisme de découverte des prix. Par conséquent, on pourrait envisager des stratégies de migration qui favorisent également les émetteurs qui se sont clairement engagés à réduire leurs émissions de gaz à effet de serre. Les stratégies de migration peuvent être appliquées au niveau des secteurs, des entreprises ou des obligations. Notre traduction].

Il est intéressant de remarquer que le terme *tilting*, à l'instar de *tapering* et *QE*, n'apparaît que dans les sessions de Questions /Réponses des Conférences de Christine Lagarde. Lors de la Conférence du 2 février 2023, Christine Lagarde affirme que tout en étant d'accord avec la stratégie de *tilting*, elle met en garde contre les risques de devenir complice dans des stratégies d'éco-blanchiment :

> It will be on the basis of that analysis, our own, and also reliable analysis that will be provided by experts that we will orientate our portfolio with a stronger tilting than we had so far. But we will be very attentive, because we should not be accomplice to greenwashing, and it's a risk-management principle that we have to comply with. [C'est sur la base de cette analyse, la nôtre et celle, fiable, qui sera fournie par des experts, que nous orienterons notre portefeuille de façon plus marquée par rapport à ce que nous avons fait jusqu'à présent. Mais nous serons très attentifs, car nous ne devons pas être complices de l'écoblanchiment,

et c'est un principe de gestion des risques auquel nous devons nous conformer. Notre traduction].

Nous pouvons parler dans ce cas aussi d'une volonté de dédramatisation des effets d'une éventuelle fin des achats de titres avec un effet supplémentaire par rapport à l'expression euphémisante du « recalibrage » : l'ajout des contours écologiques dans la politique d'achats de titres.

Tapering et *recalibrage*, entre énonciation euphémique et métonymie

La base théorique et méthodologique de notre travail se fonde sur une conception des tropes, considérés non plus comme simple ornement mais comme partie intégrante de l'expression linguistique et de l'interaction communicative, au service de la compréhension. Les figures, en tant que formes de valorisation des ressources linguistiques et non pas en tant que formes de la substitution ou de la transgression, peuvent se situer sur le plan de l'expression, telles que l'assonance ou le rythme, ou sur le plan du contenu – c'est le cas des métaphores et des métonymies – ou de l'échange communicationnel. C'est le cas de l'hyperbole et de l'ironie (Prandi, 2021 : 3). Lors de nos publications précédentes nous avons analysé le rôle dans la presse de ces figures à forte valeur argumentative: que l'on pense à la métonymie de la monnaie-hélicoptère qui devient représentative « d'une théorie économique qui prévoit un financement aux ménages, sans l'entremise des banques » et qui appartient à juste titre à l'isotopie « L'argent est un liquide ». Ou encore à l'essaim métaphorique engendré par l'isotopie « Le QE est une arme » qui fait que cet outil de politique d'expansion monétaire soit assimilé à de l'« artillerie lourde », à un « bazooka » ou à la « Grande Bertha » (Maldussi, 2020 : 131–135).

Nous classifions *recalibrage* parmi les « [e]uphemistic expressions based on conceptual metonymy » [expressions euphémiques basées sur la métonymie conceptuelle, notre traduction] (Moritz, 2018 : 57) et nous considérons la métonymie conceptuelle « as a cognitive mechanism underlying the formation of euphemistic expressions » [« comme un mécanisme cognitif qui est à la base de la formation d'expressions euphémiques ». Notre traduction] (Moritz, 2018 : 58). Le cas envisagé ici est celui de l'effet (*recalibrating*) pour la cause (*tapering* ou baisse graduelle des achats). Il est intéressant de remarquer que la configuration discursive « contraint souvent la réception de métonymies » (Bonhomme, 2006 : 94). En effet, la configuration dans laquelle s'insère la réponse de Christine Lagarde qui prévoit en tant que préambule la citation de la phrase symbole de Madame Thatcher, fonctionne en tant que signal de la part de l'énonciateur qui balise « ostensiblement l'interprétation métonymique à effectuer » (Bonhomme, 2006). En outre, comme le montre l'échange verbal entre Christine Lagarde et le journaliste, « même si le mot doux [*recalibrage*] sert à épargner la mention dure ou brutale [*tapering*], il n'empêche que les deux expressions peuvent à l'occasion se manifester dans un entourage relativement proche » (López Díaz, 2018 : 28). Ce qui montre, comme l'écrit la même auteure (2018 : 30) reprenant une idée de Allan et Burridge (1991: 28), que « ce n'est pas tellement le mot en soi qui est euphémique ou dysphémique, mais la manière dont il en est fait usage ».

L'euphémisme selon Bonhomme (2006 : 160) « repose sur deux opérations conjointes : la conversion discursive en axiologie positive d'un énoncé portant sur une réalité problématique et l'atténuation de la force de cet énoncé. En d'autres termes, l'euphémisme est un acte de parole réévaluatif, détensif et socialisé face à un référent à risque ». La métonymie, ajoute Bonhomme (2006) qui cite Pauwels (1999), « convient parfaitement au processus de l'euphémisme ». Le *recalibrage* prévoit aussi une interprétation métonymique clôturante car « [...] suite à sa forte préconstruction, [il] provoque une identification rapide et des inférences limitées chez ses énonciateurs » (Bonhomme, 2006 : 90). En outre, la métonymie « fonctionne sur des matrices préétablies qui en facilitent la reconnaissance » (Bonhomme, 2006, qui cite Prandi, 2002).

De son côté, Christine Lagarde offre à chaque fois des raisons qui justifient le *recalibrage*, comme dans l'exemple suivant :

> <u>If, on the other hand favourable financing conditions cannot be preserved, as the pace of purchase has been decided, we will adjust upward. And if the envelope is not sufficient, then we will recalibrate the entire envelope.</u> So, I can't be clearer than that. It's really identified with a very high degree of flexibility and the capacity to adjust, because we are prepared to adjust all our instruments, not just the pace of purchases. We're prepared to adjust all instruments (Conférence du 21 Janvier 2021, Session des Questions/Réponses, c'est nous qui soulignons). [Si, en revanche, des conditions de financement favorables ne peuvent être préservées, le rythme des achats ayant été décidé, nous adapterons à la hausse. <u>Et si l'enveloppe</u>

> n'est pas suffisante, dans ce cas nous recalibrerons l'ensemble de l'enveloppe. Je ne peux donc pas être plus claire. Il s'agit véritablement d'un degré très élevé de flexibilité et de capacité d'ajustement, car nous sommes prêts à adapter tous nos instruments, et pas seulement le rythme des achats. Nous sommes prêts à adapter tous les instruments. Notre traduction].

L'euphémisme, selon la définition d'Allan et Burridge (1991 : 11) est utilisé en tant qu'alternative à une « dispreferred expression, in order to avoid possible loss of face: either one's own face, or though giving offense, that of the audience, or of some third party » [« expression inadéquate, afin d'éviter de perdre la face: soit sa propre face, soit, en cas d'offense, celle de l'auditoire ou d'une tierce personne ». Notre traduction]. Burridge (2006 : 455) précise que « [w]hat is described here as 'a dispreferred expression' is one that is not desired or appropriate on a given occasion. Typically it denotes a taboo topic and so might alternatively be called 'a taboo term'» [« Ce qui est décrit ici comme 'une expression inadéquate' est une expression qui n'est pas souhaitée ou appropriée dans une occasion donnée. Typiquement, elle dénote un sujet tabou et pourrait donc être appelée 'un terme tabou' ». Notre traduction].

L'euphémisme, aussi bien que la litote, sont deux stratégies d'atténuation (Jaubert, 2008). Les deux figures se présentent :

> comme des infractions à la maxime de quantité. [Elles] ne faussent pas complètement la réalité de la chose, mais [elles] n'en disent pas tout. L'euphémisme, dans sa manifestation la plus traditionnelle, substitue à un terme cru, et aux représentations dysphoriques qui lui sont attachées, un terme du même domaine notionnel (l'interlocuteur doit pouvoir s'y retrouver), mais qui joue sur l'extension, et corollairement sur l'intension du référent, avec un substitut hyperonyme ne conservant que les traits sémantiques neutres du terme adéquat (*intervention* pour *opération*). Il peut jouer aussi directement sur l'intension avec un substitut mélioratif (les *Euménides*, ou les *moyens innocents* de Figaro). Quoi qu'il en soit l'euphémisme rogne sur l'information, que notre connaissance des référents visés permet de rétablir immédiatement (Jaubert, 2008 : 110–11).

Comme nous l'avons vu, *tapering* s'avère être un euphémisme néosémique dont la fonction est de « dissimuler des réalités qu'on ne veut pas nommer directement pour de multiples raisons » (Sablayrolles, 2016 : 188) mais finit par se transformer en mot taboo. Du reste, « [l]e lien de l'euphémisme à la néologie est indéniable, d'autant plus que l'on a pu considérer non seulement que l'euphémisme développe l'innovation linguistique mais encore que l'euphémisme neuf 'n'est que le seul et vrai euphémisme' » (Jamet & Jobert, 2010 : 14, cités par López Díaz, 2016 : 242) étant donné que l'euphémisme, comme le néologisme en général, « peut rester éphémère ou entrer dans le lexique commun de la langue et perdre ainsi chemin faisant son statut » (López Díaz, 2016). Or, comme le souligne cette même auteure « [l]'euphémisme néologique établit une catégorisation autre du réel : le signe a son signifiant et son signifié, ainsi que son référent habituel qui reste virtuel » (López Díaz, 2016 : 248) : ce qui fait que si son référent virtuel de « diminution graduelle » évoque l'idée d'une diminution sans conséquences immédiates ou violentes au vu de sa gradualité presque innocente, le référent réel, au contraire, du moins pour les partisans du *QE*, évoque une situation potentiellement néfaste, que le choix du terme *tapering* se charge de rendre moins néfaste.

Or, qu'en est-il du détour métonymique euphémisant du *recalibrage*? Du coup, penser que l'euphémisme se réduise à une pure stratégie de l'atténuation nous a paru réducteur. En particulier, si cet euphémisme s'insère à l'intérieur d'une politique qui vise la communication d'indications prospectives sur l'orientation future de la politique monétaire. Comme le souligne Kacprzak (2022 : 210–211) une reformulation consiste en:

> un mieux-dire (qui peut consister notamment à exprimer le même contenu plus exactement ou plus correctement, mais sans doute aussi à adapter la parole aux besoins voire aux attentes de l'audience), [...] qui d'une part peut servir à euphémiser pour contourner une réalité jugée trop brutale, d'autre part [est souvent utilisé] pour « déseuphémiser » le déjà-dit, quelle que soit la raison de cette dernière opération. Étant donné que la reformulation est nécessairement basée sur une différence entre l'élément source et l'élément cible, elle ne constitue pas une simple répétition.

La réponse de Christine Lagarde consiste en une euphémisation du *tapering*, une sorte de prise de distance qui lui permet de mettre sous un nouveau jour l'objet néfaste qu'est devenu le *tapering*, en le contredisant et en l'orientant positivement afin d'éviter toute sorte d'accusation sur son mandat. À l'instar de Burridge (2006 : 457), nous définissons cette création euphémistique comme une modification sémantique du type « elevation » :

> Elevation involves the substitution of words with more pleasing connotations. For example, crafted implies that something has been produced meticulously and probably by hand and is more positive than made or manufactured, blend is more positive than mixture, standard more positive than average. [La valorisation

implique la substitution de mots avec d'autres mots aux connotations plus agréables. Par exemple, 'crafted' implique que quelque chose a été produit soigneusement et probablement à la main et présente une connotation plus positive que 'made' ou 'manufactured', 'blend' est plus positif que 'mixture', 'standard' est plus positif que 'average'. Notre traduction].

L'euphémisme, nous rappelle Prandi (2021 : 229–232), occupe une place particulière dans l'espace du jeu communicationnel. Il s'agit avant tout d'une grandeur graduée: les deux pôles sont constitués par l'euphémisme extrême, le seul qui rompt le pacte communicationnel de façon unilatérale car il présuppose de tromper l'interlocuteur en cachant la vérité des choses, et l'euphémisme atténué, qui n'est qu'un pacte tacite de complicité. Or, dans le cas du *recalibrage* nous pensons qu'au vu de notre analyse ce détour métonymique de type euphémistique est finalisé à la médiation. Du reste, Bonhomme (2012 : 79–80) avait déjà mis en évidence le rôle perlocutoire de cette forme d'euphémisme « lorsqu'[elle] renforce l'harmonie entre son énonciateur et le public auquel [elle] s'adresse [...] dans le souci de ne pas choquer son allocutaire en écartant les menaces à son encontre ». Bonhomme cite à ce propos le cas des infirmes « requalifiés en 'personnes à mobilité réduite' ». Or, ajoute le même auteur, « [p]lus largement et sur un plan national, les euphémismes soudent la cohésion des citoyens autour d'une vision optimiste et solidaire »: *recalibrage* est un terme rassurant qui s'insère parfaitement dans la politique des annonces concernant la politique des achats de titres et le rythme de ces derniers. Un détour qui, s'appuyant sur la sincérité du locuteur et sur son autorité reconnue et acceptée, est continuellement mis en adéquation avec l'analyse effectuée au début des conférences.

Tapering et *recalibrage* à l'épreuve de la presse francophone

Nous procéderons brièvement à quelques remarques concernant le comportement de *tapering* et de *recalibrage* dans la presse francophone. Nous allons commencer par ce dernier. *Recalibrage*, contrairement à *QE*, n'est pas chargé culturellement (Maldussi, 2019) ce qui explique que ce terme n'est ni suivi par une glose explicative ni anticipé par une traduction paraphrastique. Ce qui montre, à notre avis, que le concept relationnel de *recalibrage* est aisément accessible. La seule fois où l'emprunt intégral *recalibrating* anticipe ou accompagne *recalibrage* est quand la réplique de

Christine Lagarde en langue anglaise est reprise dans son intégralité dans la presse française. En revanche, *recalibrage* est placé entre guillemets dans 15 occurrences sur 35, ce qui représente un clin d'œil à la célèbre réponse de Christine Lagarde.

Passons maintenant à l'analyse de *tapering*. Comme nous l'avons souligné au début de notre article, *tapering* ne figure que dans les sessions de Questions/Réponses. Ces dernières sont proposées en la seule langue anglaise. La traduction de *tapering* figure dans la base de données *FranceTerme*. L'équivalent proposé est celui de « désexpansion monétaire » (J.O. du 07/12/2018), suivi de la définition suivante: « Réduction, par paliers successifs, du volume d'achat d'actifs par une banque centrale, annonçant la fin de la politique d'expansion monétaire qu'elle menait jusqu'alors » (FranceTerme, 2018). Si d'une part l'équivalent proposé par *FranceTerme* ne figure pas dans notre sous-corpus de presse en ligne, d'autre partl'exploration de ce dernier fait état de résultats assez intéressants concernant la cohorte métalinguistique qui entoure les 118 occurrences du terme *tapering* :

- l'emprunt intégral *tapering* n'est précisé par une traduction littérale en fonction appositive qu'en cinq occurrences sur 118 : « diminution graduelle » (deux occurrences) ; « réduction progressive des achats », « dégressif », « resserrement quantitatif » (une occurrence) ;
- *tapering* est suivi d'une glose explicative ou de sa définition en sept occurrences : « Le tapering est une action d'une banque centrale qui vise à diminuer ses actifs sur un marché » ;
- *tapering* est anticipé, dans toutes les autres occurrences, par une traduction paraphrastique avec une fonction explicative au début de chaque article : « Le ralentissement progressif des achats de titres par la banque centrale (tapering) [...] ». L'emprunt intégral *tapering* est principalement utilisé dans le corps de chaque article en tant que reprise anaphorique du contexte explicatif précédent.

Notre conclusion est que *tapering*, par rapport par exemple à *QE*, un syntagme qui appelle une cohorte de formulations méta sémiques dans le discours de presse (Maldussi, 2019), présente un décodage plus prévisible car il nécessite, dans la grande majorité des cas, une seule intégration en tant que glose anticipée. Cette prévisibilité pourrait être due au fait que le sujet du *tapering* est connu depuis 2013, année de sa création par Ben Bernanke. En ce qui concerne le recours à l'emprunt intégral *tapering* dans le discours de presse, nous sommes d'accord avec ce qu'écrit Sablayrolles, à savoir qu'une :

> [a]utre manière de ne pas dire directement les choses consiste à recourir à des emprunts. D'une part, ces mots ne sont pas (sémi-) motivés dans la langue cible s'ils le sont souvent dans la langue source. D'autre part, c'est indiquer que les réalités négatives ainsi dénommées ne sont pas autochtones, mais viennent de l'extérieur, avec l'importation de mauvaises influences qui introduisent des réalités qui ne peuvent pas venir de chez soi. Ainsi, la 'bonne' qualité des locuteurs de la langue cible reste intacte (Sablayrolles, 2016 : 196–197)[11].

Or,

> [l]a non- motivation en langue cible d'un emprunt s'accompagne d'un type particulier de motivation : la forme étrangère dit l'origine étrangère de la chose. Ce n'est sans doute pas par hasard qu'il n'y a guère eu de tentatives de trouver des équivalents français à *kidnapping*, *pickpocket* etc. Le maintien de la forme étrangère est signifiant et tend à dégager la responsabilité de la population autochtone qui ne fait que subir de mauvaises influences extérieures. Cette atténuation de la responsabilité relève de l'euphémisme (Sablayrolles, 2016 : 199)[12].

Une atténuation qui ne manque pas de soulever continuellement des polémiques et qui donne lieu, comme l'atteste notre sous-corpus de presse, à une situation de polyphonie divergente (Bonhomme, 2020): en fin de compte, le *tapering* ne serait-il pas une « une réalité camouflée », une

---

11 À propos des autres manières de ne pas dire directement les choses, Sablayrolles nomme, entre autres, les périphrases, les changements d'emploi, la renomination, la pluralisation non pluralisante telle que dans l'exemple 'Les quartiers' pour indiquer les quartiers défavorisés etc. (Sablayrolles, 2016 : 191–195).

12 En ce qui concerne la maîtrise de la langue source, Sablayrolles écrit que « [l]'absence de motivation de mots dérivés ou composés importés vaut bien sûr pour les gens ignorant la langue source ou ne la maîtrisant qu'imparfaitement. Elle peut être moindre ou effacée pour ceux qui la connaissent bien, mais cela reste néanmoins démotivé dans le système de la langue cible ». Le même auteur parle à ce propos d'un « double éloignement par rapport à ce que serait une dénomination (sémi-) motivée en langue autochtone » (Sablayrolles, 2016 : 197).

diminution des achats ayant effectivement eu lieu? En tout cas « il ne faut pas le dire: le mot fait peur » (Wenger, 2021, en ligne).

Conclusions

Les termes *QE* et *tapering* partagent plusieurs caractéristiques: ils n'apparaissent que dans les sessions des Questions/ Réponses et sont réunis par le fait de se transformer en tabous dans l'interaction verbale. Ce qui confirme la thèse de López Díaz (2018 : 28) selon qui tabous et euphémismes peuvent coexister « dans un entourage relativement proche ». *QE*, né en tant qu'expression opaque, trouve un terrain fertile aux États-Unis et se transforme en instrument de pression en Europe à l'encontre de la *BCE*. *Tapering* naît, au contraire, en tant qu'euphémisme et devient tabou au moment où il devient le symbole d'une politique monétaire moins accommodante. Les détracteurs de la *BCE* ne cessent de rappeler qu'ils sont en faveur d'une réduction, voire d'un arrêt complet des achats de titres, ce qui provoque la métonymie euphémisante du recalibrage de la part de Christine Lagarde.

L'euphémisme désamorce le tabou, le rend inoffensif, voire acceptable. De plus, dans ce cas d'espèces, la perspective concernant ses effets, grâce à un procédé de type sémantique, de négative devient positive : le *recalibrage*, connoté positivement car il ne prévoit pas le sème de la réduction ou de la rupture abrupte, focalise plutôt une redistribution heureuse qui sera effectuée au vu de la situation économique de la zone euro et devrait permettre à Christine Lagarde d'obtenir un soutien politique à son mandat.

Nous pensons, en conclusion, que la dédramatisation induite par l'euphémisme qualifie ce dernier plutôt comme une figure de la médiation par excellence. Si nous projetons cette attitude dans le cadre de la politique inaugurée par Draghi, qui est celle de la politique des annonces, l'euphémisme s'avère plutôt comme une figure de la médiation fonctionnelle à cette dernière, dont les objectifs ne se situent pas dans le présent de l'action mais plutôt dans le moyen et dans le long terme. L'euphémisme devient alors l'arme par excellence de la stratégie des annonces pour gérer les attentes et les craintes à court terme des investisseurs, afin d'atteindre un objectif à plus long terme. Du reste, comme l'écrit Betbèze (2021, en ligne),

« [c]es mêmes inquiétudes se retrouvent à chaque conférence de Christine Lagarde, la présidente de la BCE, toujours interrogée sur son plan de quantitative easing de 100 milliards d'euros par mois » et les réponses aux questions « [a]llez-vous pouvoir continuer vos achats de papiers européens en respectant les règles que la BCE s'est donnée pour ne pas acheter trop de papiers italiens? Comment allez-vous résister aux pressions allemandes et résister aussi à la hausse des taux longs qui viendrait des Etats-Unis? », visiblement ne vont pas changer : « il n'y a aucun problème, nous sommes dans nos mandats, rappelez-nous plus tard. Surtout, pas de tantrum! ».

Bibliographie

Allan, K. et Burridge, K. (1991). *Euphemism and dysphemism: Language used as shield and weapon.* New York: Oxford University Press.

Blinder, A. (2001). *How do central banks talk?. Centre for Economic Policy Research.* Studies, International Center for Monetary and Banking.

Bonhomme, M. (2006). *Le discours métonymique.* Berne : Peter Lang.

Bonhomme, M. (2012). La réception de l'euphémisme: entre réussite et échec interactif. In M. Bonhomme, M. de La Torre et A. Horak (Éds.), *Études pragmatico-discursives sur l'euphémisme* (pp. 73–88). Frankfurt am Main: Peter Lang.

Bonhomme, M. (2020). Polyphonie divergente et mise en cause des euphémismes dans la presse écrite. In M. López Díaz et A. Seoane (Éds.), Les euphémismes dans les médias: entre voilements, démasquages et discours qui les traversent. *Çédille, revista de estudios franceses*, 17: 25–43.

Burridge, K. (2006). Taboo, euphemism, and political correctness. *Encyclopedia of Language & Linguistics*, deuxième édition, 455–462.

Gallie, W. (1956). Essentially contested concepts. *Proceeding of the Aristotelian Society*, 56: 167–198.

Golder, Y. (2019). *Margaret Thatcher: Construction d'une image politique, 1950–1990.* Linguistique. Université de Strasbourg, thèse doctorale.

Jamet, D. et Jobert, M. (2010). Juste un petit mot sur l'euphémisme... In D. Jamet et M. Jobert (Éds.), *Empreintes de l'euphémisme. Tours et détours* (pp. 11–28). Paris: L'Harmattan.

Jaubert, A. (2008). Dire et plus ou moins dire. Analyse pragmatique de l'euphémisme et de la litote. *Langue Française,* 160: 105–116.

Kacprzak, A. (2022). De l'euphémisme « mis à nu » par la reformulation. *Studia Neophilologica,* 94(2): 210–220.

López Díaz, M. (2016). Euphémismes néosémiques au sujet de l'emploi en temps de crise. *La Linguistique,* 52(2): 239–256.

López Díaz, M. (2018). La cooccurrence du tabou et de l'euphémisme ou les conditions de la synonymie. *Travaux de linguistique,* 1(76): 27–42.

Maldussi, D. (2015). Aspetti propedeutici della traduzione economico-finanziaria: l'orientamento alla futurità nell'informativa societaria, tra effetti perlocutivi, inferenze predittive ed implicitezza. In F. Gatta (Éd.), *L'italiano delle professioni: ricerca, traduzione, didattica, Mediazioni* (pp. 1–30, Vol. 18).

Maldussi, D. (2019). Aspects perlocutoires, discursifs et traductionnels dans la terminologie de la BCE. Un regard croisé franco-italien. In F. Barbin et S. Monjean-Decaudin (Éds.), *La traduction juridique et économique. Aspects théoriques et pratiques* (pp. 85–97). Paris: Classiques Garnier.

Maldussi, D. (2020). Guerre des isotopies dans la conceptualisation de la néologie d'emprunt: le 'quantitative easing' de la BCE et sa figuralité à l'épreuve du discours de presse francophone. In J. C. de Hoyos, C. Poix, A. Renwick et C. Veleanu (Éds.), *Défis de la néologie en langues romanes au XXIe siècle/Desafíos de la neología en las lenguas románicas en el siglo XXI* (pp. 125–138). Murcia: EDITUM, Ediciones de la Universidad de Murcia.

Moritz, I. (2018). Metonymy-based euphemisms in war-related speeches by George W. Bush and Barack Obama. In A. Pizarro (Éd.), *Linguistic Taboo Revisited: Novel Insights from Cognitive Perspectives* (pp. 55–78). Berlin-Boston: Mouton De Gruyter.

Orioli, A. (2016). *Gli oracoli della moneta. L'arte della parola nel linguaggio dei banchieri centrali.* Bologna: Il Mulino.

Pauwels, P. (1999). Putting metonymy in its place. In K. Panther et G. Radden (Éds.), *Metonymy in language and thought* (pp. 255–273). Amsterdam-Philadelphia: John Benjamins.

Prandi, M. (2002). Métonymie et métaphore ; parcours partagés dans l'espace de la communication. *Semen,* 15: 71–82.

Prandi, M. (2021). *Le metafore tra le figure: una mappa ragionata.* Torino: UTET Università.

Sablayrolles, J.-F. (2016). Des procédés néologiques euphémiques et quelques domaines privilégiés d'apparition. *La Linguistique,* 52(2): 187–200.

Articles de presse en ligne

Betbèze, J.-P. (2021). *Le spectre d'un « taper tantrum »*, https://www.optionfinance.fr/analyses/le-spectre-dun-taper-tantrum.html.

Longo, M. (2021). Quanto vale l'effetto Draghi sullo spread? Un miliardo di risparmi potenziali, *Il Sole 24 Ore* du 6 février, https://24plus.ilsole24ore.com/art/quanto-vale-l-effetto-draghi-spread-miliardo-risparmi-potenziali-ADTzN5HB.

Schnabel, I. (2021). From market neutrality to market efficiency, Discours de bienvenue au symposium de la DG Recherche de la BCE *Climate change, financial markets and green growth*, Frankfurt am Main, le 14 juin j. https://www.ecb.europa.eu/press/key/date/2021/html/ecb.sp210614~162bd7c253.en.html.

Wenger, P. (2021). *Les taperings sont une réalité camouflée.* LesEchos investir https://investir.lesechos.fr/marches-indices/economie-politique/les-taperings-sont-une-realite-camouflee-1850582.

Sitographie

Adviseonly. (2021). *ABCFinanza: Cos'è il Tapering e perché se ne parla.* https:// www.adv iseo nly.com/ cap ire- la- fina nza/ abc- fina nza/ abc fina nza- cose- il- taper ing- e- per che- se- ne- parla/ (dernière consultation le 10.09.2023).

Affaritaliani.it. (2021). *Bce, falchi all'attacco: ma quale inflazione temporanea, preparare fine Pepp.* https:// www.affari tali ani.it/ econo mia/ bce-falchi-all-attacco-ma-quale-inflazione-temporanea-preparare-fine-pepp-755547.html (dernière consultation le 10.09.2023).

Banque de France. (2021). *Le quantitative easing.* https://abc-economie.banque-france.fr/quantitative-easing (dernière consultation le 10.09.2023).

BCE. (2017). *Qu'est-ce que la forward guidance?* https://www.ecb.europa.eu/ecb/educational/explainers/tell-me/html/what-is-forward_guidance.fr.html (dernière consultation le 14.07.2023).

Cambridge Dictionary. *Taper*. https ://dictionary.cambridge.org/dictionary/english/taper?q=To+taper (dernière consultation le 10.09.2023).

FranceTerme. (2018). *Tapering*. https://www.culture.fr/franceterme/terme/ECON1481 (dernière consultation le 10.09.2023).

Investopedia. (2020). *Taper Tantrum of 2013 : What it is and what caused it*. https://www.investopedia.com/terms/t/taper-tantrum.asp (dernière consultation le 27.07.2023).

OptionFinance. (2021). *La réduction des achats d'actifs ne signifie pas que les taux vont s'envoler*. https://www.optionfinance.fr/dossiers-partenaires/la-reduction-des-achats-dactifs-ne-signifie-pas-que-les-taux-vont-senvoler.html (dernière consultation le 10.07.2023).

Oxford Advanced Learner's Dictionary. (2023). *Tilt*. https:// www.oxfordlearnersdictionaries.com/definition/english/tilt_1?q=tilt (dernière consultation le 10.07.2023).

Treccani. (2020). *Whatever it takes*. https://www.treccani.it/vocabolario/whatever-it-takes_(Neologismi) (dernière consultation le 10.06.2023).

Wikipédia. (2023). *Taux directeur*. https://fr.wikipedia.org/wiki/Taux_directeur (dernière consultation le 10.07.2023).

www.ingramcontent.com/pod-product-compliance
Ingram Content Group UK Ltd.
Pitfield, Milton Keynes, MK11 3LW, UK
UKHW041827031026
15587UKWH00002B/613

9 783631 913802